Business FOR *Care* *Management*

A GUIDE TO COSTING, CONTRACTING AND NEGOTIATING

Penny Mares

AGE Concern

BOOKS

© 1996 Penny Mares
Published by Age Concern England
1268 London Road
London SW16 4ER

Editor Caroline Hartnell
Design and production Eugenie Dodd Typographics
Copy preparation Vinnette Marshall

Printed and bound in Great Britain by Bell & Bain Ltd, Glasgow

A catalogue record for this book is available from the British Library

ISBN 0–86242–191–8

All rights reserved; no part of this work may be reproduced
in any form, by mimeograph or any other means,
without permission in writing from the publisher.

Contents

About the author

Penny Mares is an established writer and trainer on health and social issues. She has written a range of educational materials for professionals in the caring services. She is co-author of *Health Care in Multiracial Britain*, published by the National Extension College, and *Home for Good*, an information and training pack on living conditions and community care, published by Care and Repair. She is author of two BBC training guides for professionals working with carers, *Who Cares?* and *Who Cares Now?*, to accompany training videos based on the TV series of the same name.

Penny has also written a number of books for people caring at home, including *You and Caring*, published by the King's Fund, *Caring in a Crisis: Caring for someone who is dying*, published by ACE Books, and, with Nancy Kohner, *Who Cares Now?*, the BBC handbook on caring at home for an older person.

Penny worked in the public and voluntary sector until she became a free-lance writer and trainer in 1987, when she had to set about acquiring many of the basic business skills discussed in this book.

Acknowledgements

I would especially like to thank David Best, Community Care Consultant and Associate Age Concern Trainer, Linda Gregory and Bob Revell for their helpful advice and comments on what should go into this book; Roger Fox, Bronwen Holden, and Lynn Wilce for discussing with me their experiences of the reforms as front-line workers; Philip Coyne for help with research and advice on presentation of financial issues; and Evelyn McEwen, Bob Anderson and Helen Dickens for reviewing the first draft.

I would also like to thank all the other people who offered ideas, information or advice, including Jan Burrows, Jill Chapman, Cath Birch, Paul Cambridge, Tim Clarke, John England, Janet Fisher, Gerry McCabe, John Lennon, Judith North, Pat Steele, and Pam Walters and her colleagues at Wakefield Social Services, all of whom gave up time to discuss the information needs of front-line workers with me.

I am grateful to Barbara Meredith for permission to draw on material from *The Community Care Handbook* (2nd edition 1995), published by ACE Books, especially in Chapter 1 and pp 119–121 'Where community care money comes from'. Chapter 3 and Chapter 7 (pp 124–126 'Costing the care package') draw on material in *Devising and Resourcing Personal Care Packages* (1995) by Flora Gathorne-Hardy, available from Disablement Income Group, Unit 5, Archway Business Centre, 19–23 Wedmore Street, London N19 4RZ, and I am grateful to DIG for permission to adapt ideas from this useful booklet.

I would also like to thank the following for permission to reproduce or adapt material.

The table on p 24, 'Qualifications accepted for care manager posts', is adapted from research by Buckinghamshire Social Services Department, September 1995. The diagram on p 34, 'Managing care in the community', is adapted from North Yorkshire Community Care Plan, County Module, 1994–95, p 25 (diagram titled 'Commissioning'). The diagram on pp 36–37, 'Full separation of purchasing and providing roles', is reproduced from *GNVQ Advanced Health and Social Care* (2nd edition 1995) Liam Clarke, Bruce Sachs and Sue Ford, published by Stanley Thornes, p 266 (Figure 10.2 'The structure of a typical social services department'). The diagram on pp 36–37, 'Separation of purchasing and providing roles at a lower level', is reprinted by kind permission of Heinemann Educational, a division of Reed Education and Professional Publishing Ltd, from *Advanced Health and Social Care*, Heinemann GNVQ, 1995, edited by Neil Moonie, p 139 (Figure 7.9 'Example of a local authority social services department'). The table on p 94, 'Balancing clarity, flexibility and necessary detail', uses examples adapted from *Guidance on Contracting for Domiciliary and Day Care Services* (1995) Association of Metropolitan Authorities, Association of County Councils and Association of Directors of Social Services, pp 53–54. Appendix 2: 'Example of an individual service contract for the purchase of domiciliary care services' and Appendix 3: 'Example of a service specification for domiciliary care services' are also reproduced from the same document by kind permission of the Association of Metropolitan Authorities. Some examples in the section on 'Specifying individual care needs' on pp 97–102 are adapted from *Guidance on the use of the requisition for care document to specify service user needs*, produced by Rotherham Social Services Department. Parts of Chapter 8 draw on *It's a Deal: A practical negotiation handbook* (1989) Paul Steele, John Murphy and Richard Russill, McGraw Hill; the table on p 143 is adapted from p 66 (Figure 6.3 'Phases of the negotiation'). The action plan format on pp 158–159 is adapted from *The Emotional Effects of Childbirth* (1995) May Johnstone, The Marcé Society, pp 94–95. The diagram on p 162, 'Resources for community care', is adapted from *Care in the Community – Five years on* (1994) Paul Cambridge et al, Arena, p 81 (Figure 8.1, diagram 2 'New inter-agency working'). The checklist of community care resources for older people on pp 163–164 is adapted from *Caring in a Crisis: What to do and who to turn to* (1993) Marina Lewycka, ACE Books.

Penny Mares

April 1996

Note on terminology

Care management, care manager

Care management means widely different things in different local authorities. If you are involved in needs-led assessment, care planning, arranging or purchasing services for individual users, and monitoring or reviewing their care, you are involved in care management.

In some local authorities, the title of 'care manager' is reserved for qualified professionals who assess and arrange services for users with complex care needs. In many authorities, the front-line workers who assess needs and buy care for older people are drawn from a range of backgrounds. Some have a professional or vocational qualification, others have not. At present, some local authorities do not use the term 'care management' at all to describe the activities of assessing needs and arranging care.

Because the term 'care manager' has specific but often quite different meanings in different social services departments, the more general terms 'front-line worker' and 'care management staff' have been used throughout this book.

Service user, client, person needing care

'Service user' is generally used as shorthand to describe the person needing or receiving community care services. The term 'client' is sometimes used in talking about the particular relationship between the front-line worker and the person needing care. 'Service user' is a rather impersonal term, but it is neutral and avoids confusion. The term 'consumer' or 'customer' has deliberately been avoided: when local authorities purchase care on behalf of service users, it is the authority who is the customer or consumer with purchasing power, *not* the person needing care.

Mixed economy of care

This refers to the use of independent providers (ie private, not-for-profit and voluntary organisations) alongside public services. As part of the community care reforms, social services departments have a responsibility to promote a mixed economy of care in adult services. The Government's intention is to widen the range of options available to service users.

The social care market

It is the Government's view that a mixed economy of care will create a social care 'market' in which competition between providers will lead to improvements in services, as they become more consumer-conscious and cost-aware. Critics argue that competition does not *necessarily* lead to improvements in services. The social care market is sometimes referred to as a 'quasi-market' (quasi = 'as if' or 'almost') because, unlike a true market, it is closely regulated to ensure some stability in the supply of services. In a 'free' market, competition is the only regulating mechanism.

Introduction

Who is this book for?

This book is for front-line workers who are involved in care management. It aims to provide a basic introduction to the practical, administrative and financial skills that are needed to do the job well – 'business skills' for short. It will be particularly useful to practitioners and students who are new to care management and to those who are not from a social services background. It will also be useful to managers responsible for identifying the training and development needs of care management staff and to other staff involved in purchasing and providing.

If you are involved in care management, you will be aware that the 1993 changes in community care are complex and wide-ranging. One of the biggest changes, which reflects the Government's aim of promoting the independent sector, is the requirement that social services departments should buy services from private, not-for-profit and voluntary providers – so encouraging a mixed economy of care.

Tensions and dilemmas in care management

Empathy with the client is essential. So many clients have their hopes hampered by handicap or distress. The helping process, however logical, is like 'an empty gong booming' unless it has at its heart a caring concern which clients can realise and recognise. People under stress or facing a new challenge need a helper who will stimulate and motivate energies and imagination.
Assessing Needs and Planning Care in Social Work (1993)
Brian Taylor and Toni Devine

Remember that acceptance of a product or service by a customer is a result; everything else is a cost. Management is paid to get results and minimise costs, all costs.
Essentials of Business Budgeting (1995) Robert Finney

These opposing viewpoints highlight one of the main tensions built into the role of care management staff: the tension between the economic and social objectives of care management.

Buying care services for users is now part of everyday practice for many care managers, social workers, social welfare officers and social work assistants. This involves many front-line workers in 'business' activities that are entirely new to them – for example handling contracts, accurately specifying individual care needs, costing care packages, negotiating prices with providers and monitoring the quality of service that individual clients receive from independent sector providers. Local authorities' increasing financial constraints, and the impact of financial responsibility for the continuing care needs of people discharged from hospital, mean that care management staff are likely to find themselves at the sharp end of rationing resources to service users and carers.

At the same time, a crucial objective for front-line workers is to identify and meet the social needs of their clients as sensitively and appropriately as possible. If you are involved in planning and implementing care for individual clients, you need to understand purchasing systems and contracting arrangements in order to arrange services. Developing your ability to operate within the reformed market system will mean that you can help users to get the best out of it. Business skills are not an end in themselves. Unless they are used in care management to help achieve concrete improvements in the user's well-being, quality of life or quality of care, there is no point to them. Their focus should always be on the benefits to the person needing care.

How to use this book

This book has been designed so that it can be used in a number of ways. The important thing is to adapt the ideas it contains in the way that is most useful for you.

Each chapter contains:

- practical information and discussion about general principles, common practices, and variations in practice between local authorities;
- questions and checklists to help you check how much you know, think about your own practice, or develop your awareness of policies and procedures in your own authority;

■ a short list of recommended reading to enable you to expand your knowledge and awareness, with notes explaining why each publication is useful.

The final chapter is an action plan. There is space for you to make notes on topics that you would like to know more about or skills that you would like to develop further. The aim is to help you identify your personal priorities and decide what you can do about them.

What is not covered

There is enormous diversity in the way local authorities have developed and are developing care management. Care management staff are drawn from a range of backgrounds: they are mainly social workers, but there are also community nurses, occupational therapists, home care managers and other workers with experience of or a vocational qualification in social care. In different authorities care management staff are involved to different degrees in purchasing individual care packages from a range of providers in the independent sector, with differing levels of responsibility for budget management. It would be impossible to discuss all the local variations in an introductory guide like this, so limits have inevitably had to be set.

For simplicity, it has been assumed that care management is organised within the social services department. There are many variants on this arrangement, but the general principles and common practices discussed here can be applied or adapted by care management staff working in other organisations. At the end of the day, the local authority is the body that commissions and pays for social care services, wherever the care management staff are based.

The book does not discuss schemes for direct payment to people with disabilities, so that they can arrange and purchase their own care services. The Community Care (Direct Payments) Act 1996 enables certain people with disabilities to receive direct payments from social services departments so that they can purchase personal assistance to suit their individual circumstances. Some people will need additional skills and support to manage their direct payments and employ assistants. Service users' groups argue that, if the direct payments system is to work well, it is essential for local authorities to develop adequate training and support systems, to give service users the backup they need. It will be essential to monitor how the legislation works in practice.

The book tends to concentrate on services that are relatively new and developing, so there is more discussion about independent domiciliary and day care services, for example, than about more established services such as residential and nursing home care.

The illustrations and examples focus on care services for older people, but the principles discussed apply equally to other client groups.

The future

In time, the lessons learned from implementing the reformed community care system will help to shape new policy and new organisational changes. In the meantime, the effects of the reforms are far-reaching. Not everyone agrees with every part of them, but it is important that everyone involved in care management understands the skills and processes involved in buying care for individual users and, as far as possible, can use these skills to make the present system work in the best interests of their clients.

1 Care management – the background

This chapter explains the background to the changes in the way community care is organised and paid for. If you are involved in care management, you will be aware that the 1993 changes in community care are complex and far-reaching. Buying care services for users is now part of everyday practice for many front-line workers, and this involves 'business' activities such as handling contracts, negotiating prices with providers and monitoring the quality of service provided to the user. You need to understand the history of the community care reforms and the background to care management if you are to do the job well, and to make sense of some of the tensions that are part of the front-line worker's role.

The first part of this chapter briefly reviews the development of community care and of the 'mixed economy of care', as envisaged in the National Health Service and Community Care Act 1990. The second part looks at the development of care management, and at some of the dilemmas that the business side of care management can create for front-line workers.

QUESTIONS THIS CHAPTER WILL TRY TO ANSWER

■ Why did the Government change the way community care is organised and paid for?

■ Why was care management introduced?

■ Why are local authorities required to purchase a proportion of community care services from independent providers?

■ What dilemmas do care management staff face in purchasing care services for clients?

THE DEVELOPMENT OF COMMUNITY CARE

Community care has many meanings. Here it is used to mean the web of care and support provided for people with a physical or mental illness or disability by their families or other members of the community, and by public, private or voluntary services. It means helping people remain in their homes, when this is feasible and what they want, and creating home-like places with appropriate support for people who can no longer remain in their own homes.

The 1989 White Paper *Caring for People* set out the Government's objectives for the future of community care, and the changes that would be necessary to achieve these. *Caring for People* provided the framework for the NHS and Community Care Act 1990 and for policy changes which were phased in between 1991 and 1993.

The concept of community care was not, however, a new one. Government objectives drew together a number of separate strands in the debate about how community care might develop, and mapped out a particular approach to tackling them. The key issues were:

- the belief that people would prefer to be cared for in their own homes, or in smaller home-like places, rather than in large institutions;

- the problem of coordination between health and social services;

- competition for limited resources;

- the increasing costs of community care, especially nursing and residential home care for the growing elderly population.

We shall briefly look at each of these below.

The move away from institutional care

The early part of the twentieth century saw small but significant developments in some services in the community, as an alternative to institutional care, but the major change came with the welfare reforms after the Second World War. Through the 1950s and 1960s, the dehumanising effects of institutional care became more widely recognised.

In the early 1970s, proposals to improve services for people with mental illness and mental disability called for better coordination of services, and for more support for people in their own homes. Debate about how this could best be achieved continued through the seventies and eighties, and continues today.

Coordination between health and social services

An important strand in the development of community care is the belief that organisational change and closer collaboration between the providers of health and social care can lead to improvements in services. The late 1960s and early 1970s saw a restructuring of social services, followed in 1974 by a new National Health Service structure and local government reorganisation. Since then a major debate in the development of community care has been about how to improve coordination between health and social services.

The 1990 reforms introduced the most significant changes in the organisation of health and social care in the last 50 years. By changing the funding structure and introducing care management, the Government hoped both to improve the coordination and flexibility of services and to control costs.

Competing priorities

In the health services, acute and non-acute services (that is, services for people with chronic or continuing needs) compete for resources, and the less glamorous non-acute services often lose out. The duty to provide childcare services has made increasing demands on social services resources over the years, during a period when central government has sought to curb or reduce public spending. For most social services departments, this has meant shrinking resources to meet the needs of adult client groups.

During the 1980s, concern about ever-increasing demand for health and social care fuelled the debate about the need to target resources. The principle of *universal* provision, available as of right and according to need, was questioned. The Government argued that provision should be *selective*, dependent on means and limited to those in greatest need.

Targeting resources was also a way of controlling the rising costs of community care.

Increasing costs

By the mid-1980s, the Government was becoming concerned about the increasing cost of residential and nursing home care for the growing elderly population, and cited evidence of abuse in the level of fees charged in some areas. A national system of fees was introduced in 1985. This was followed in 1986 by the Audit Commission report, *Making a Reality of Community Care*, which suggested that the availability of Supplementary Benefit payments for residential and nursing home care was creating a 'perverse incentive' to admit people to care homes when, in many cases, it would cost less to help them to remain in their own homes. This led the Government to ask Sir Roy Griffiths to look at the organisation and funding of community care services with a view to controlling costs and increasing efficiency. (At the time of the Audit Commission report, there was evidence that for people with more complex needs, adequate community care would *not* be a cheaper solution. Critics of the Government's approach to community care have continued to argue that community care cannot work unless it is adequately funded.)

The Griffiths report

The 1988 Griffiths report, *Community Care: Agenda for action*, made a number of recommendations for action which were to become the baseline for the changes set out in the 1989 White Paper and the NHS and Community Care Act 1990. The table below shows how the key recommendations in the Griffiths report were put into practice.

GRIFFITHS RECOMMENDATIONS	CHANGES IN PRACTICE
Public resources should be targeted on those in greatest need	*Introduction of needs-led assessment*
People who are able to should pay towards the cost of services provided in their own homes	*Introduction of charging policies for day and domiciliary services. (Charges are generally less than the full cost of services.)*

Local authorities should draw up plans with health and housing authorities to show how they will work together to provide community care services	*Development of community care plans and joint commissioning*
Social services authorities should have systems to identify and assess care needs, decide on an appropriate package of care, arrange delivery, and keep under review the individual's needs and the services provided	*Development of care management*
Social services should also determine the priority to be given to cases, in the light of resources available and the competing needs of others	*Development of targets, priorities, eligibility criteria, etc*
The role of the local authority should change: it should become an enabler, organising and purchasing social care services from a range of providers, rather than itself being the main provider of services	*Separation of purchasing and providing roles. Development of the mixed economy of care, or care market*

THE INTRODUCTION OF THE 'MIXED ECONOMY OF CARE'

Two objectives of the Government's community care reforms were to 'secure better value for taxpayer's money' – or control the cost to the State of welfare provision – and to 'promote the development of a flourishing independent sector' (*Caring for People*, para 1.11). The Government wished to increase the efficiency of publicly funded services, and competition between a variety of providers (ie public, private and voluntary) was considered the best way to do this. The Government's intention is that competition between providers will result in more responsive services, better value for money and increased choice for service users.

In order to promote a market in which providers would compete to supply services to local authorities, the Government introduced three major changes in the financial structure of social care services.

The transfer of Department of Social Security funds

From April 1993, some of the money that would have been spent on paying for residential and nursing home care through the social security system was transferred from the Department of Social Security (DSS) to local authorities. This is known as the 'transfer element' of the Special Transitional Grant. The purpose was to remove the incentive to place clients in care homes (which was paid for from Income Support rather than from health or social services budgets) and to make money available to provide more care in people's own homes. Local authorities were then able to use it for domiciliary, day and respite care. There has been a long and continuing debate about how the DSS calculations are made, and about whether enough money has been transferred to cover adequately local authorities' increased responsibility for arranging community care services.

Purchaser–provider separation

To develop their function as 'enabling authorities', or purchasers of care from a range of providers, the Government required local authorities to take a strategic planning role, to make a distinction between their purchasing and providing roles, and to separate the organisation of these functions within social services departments. Local authorities have approached these structural changes in widely different ways; the pattern of purchaser–provider separation thus varies from area to area and can be a source of confusion for users, workers and other agencies (see pp 35–38 for more information).

The requirement to spend STG money in the independent sector

To promote the development of the independent sector, local authorities' community care plans (see p 32) must show how they will encourage independent sector providers. Between 1993 and 1996, local authorities in

England were required to spend 85 per cent of the 'transfer element' of the Special Transitional Grant (ie money that the DSS would have spent on Income Support under the old system) on purchasing services from the independent sector. Some authorities continued to spend this on places in the independent residential and nursing homes that already existed rather than on developing independent provision of domiciliary and day care services. In 1994, therefore, the Government directed local authorities to include arrangements for purchasing non-residential care from the independent sector in their community care plans (Department of Health Circular LAC(94)12 *Community Care Plans (Independent Sector Non-residential Care) Direction*, 1994). At present, the rules for future allocation and spending of the STG are uncertain.

The mixed economy of care varies widely from area to area. The existing pattern of independent providers is very uneven: there are large numbers of care homes in seaside areas, for example, but few in inner city areas. Generally, the development of domiciliary care providers has been slower than expected. Local authorities with a strong tradition of commitment to public services have been reluctant to encourage provision by independent providers. Some authorities have enabled their own services to become established as independent not-for-profit companies or trusts to compete with private providers. In some areas (for example within authorities covering large rural areas with scattered populations), it has not been economically feasible for voluntary or private providers to develop services.

THE ROLE OF CARE MANAGEMENT

Care management is a method of tailoring services to meet individual need. The Griffiths report recommended care management as an approach to improving joint working between health and social services, and matching services more closely to needs. *Caring for People* and later Government policy and practice guidance documents (see 'Recommended reading' at the end of the chapter) fleshed out approaches to implementing care management within the reformed community care framework.

CARE MANAGEMENT – WHO DOES IT?

Care management is a process composed of six core tasks:

- deciding the level of assessment
- assessing need
- planning care
- implementing the care plan
- monitoring
- reviewing

Which of these are you involved in?
Staff who carry out care management tasks are not all called care managers, nor are they all from a social work background. A 1995 survey by *Community Care* magazine found that the majority of staff with a care management role were not in fact called care managers (*Community Care*, 30 March 1995). Assessment and care planning for older clients whose needs are not complex is often done by unqualified social work staff.

A 1995 survey of local authorities by Buckinghamshire County Council found that care management staff with professional qualifications were drawn from a wide range of training backgrounds, as shown in the table below. Sixty-four local authorities said that they required a professional qualification, but most of these considered applicants from a range of backgrounds.

Qualifications accepted for care management posts
Social work, OT and nursing 20

Social work only 17

OT and social work 11

Social work, OT, nursing and other qualification 7

Nursing and social work 2

Social work and other qualification 2

Social work, OT and other qualification 2

Social work, OT, nursing and education 2

Social work, nursing, education and other 1

Source Buckinghamshire Social Services Department, September 1995.

The concept of care management (the original term was 'case management') evolved in Canada and the USA in the 1970s and 1980s in response to concerns about fragmented services and the rising costs of long-term care in countries which did not have a universal welfare system. Care management is a way of improving coordination between services, but it need not necessarily be linked to any particular system for organising or financing service provision. It was imported to the UK through the work of the Personal Social Services Research Unit (PSSRU) at Kent University and pilot projects in several local authorities.

Care management differs from traditional casework and management of services in its emphasis on tailoring services to the individual needs of service users rather than seeking to 'fit' them into existing services.

A core task of care management is **assessment**. The traditional approach to assessment in health and social services was often piecemeal and frag-mented: different professionals might assess the same individual for dif-ferent (and often poorly coordinated) services, and little further monitoring would take place unless there were major changes in the per-son's circumstances. The care management process developed in North America, by contrast, was based on a 'holistic' assessment: the needs of the whole person, their physical and social environment, informal support networks and personal preferences are all taken into account before a package of services is planned and arranged for them. The care plan is closely monitored, and reassessment and new services are arranged if necessary.

In practice, methods of care management vary widely. Different models evolved in the USA and Canada, and various approaches are being devel-oped and adapted in countries with different systems of providing and paying for health and social care around the world.

Care management in the UK

Government guidance issued in 1991 set out five possible models or approaches, and suggested that local authorities would need to develop different models suited to the type and level of users' needs.

> A further period of experimentation will be necessary to evaluate the applica-tion of different models to the various user groups, while at the same time adhering to some common principles of care management.
>
> *Managers' Guide*, para 3.38

At the time of writing, many local authorities are going through this period of experimentation as they develop and adapt a variety of approaches to care management. Even within the UK, therefore, care management has come to mean widely different things in different authorities. At the same time as adjusting to care management methods, front-line workers in the UK have also had to get to grips with the reformed system for organising and funding care, and the emerging 'contract culture'. Training in the practical tasks and skills involved in buying care, and opportunities for discussion about the ethical questions this raises in day-to-day practice, are essential if care management arrangements are to work effectively.

Chapter 3 looks in more detail at the tasks involved in care management, and reviews the skills you need to deal with the business aspects of planning and purchasing care.

BUSINESS ASPECTS OF CARE MANAGEMENT: THE DILEMMAS

Organisational change inevitably throws up new tensions in practice, and the 1993 changes in the organisation and funding of community care have created specific dilemmas for front-line workers involved in care management. Buying care from independent providers involves balancing different interests: the needs of your client, professional responsibility and accountability, the social services department's budget limits and the provider's need to generate income. The final part of this chapter looks at three important tensions faced by care management staff and asks you to think about how these affect your day-to-day practice.

Carrying out needs-led assessment within limited budgets

Liz Perkins, Policy Studies Institute: 'There is some evidence that two care managers assessing the same person, using the same assessment form, may identify different needs and different service solutions. The reasons for this may include their preference for a particular provider, their different access to resources, their different approach to risk and their different approach to accountability' (*Caring for People Who Live at Home Newsheet*, Policy Studies Institute, Winter 1994).

The NHS and Community Care Act made assessment of need for community care services a duty for local authorities. Griffiths argued that assessment of need would enable social services departments to target resources on those whose needs were greatest (and therefore to screen out those with lesser needs).

There has been much debate about what a 'need' is and which needs should be met. In practice, each social services department develops its own **eligibility criteria** for services. These criteria are determined by existing resources (services and funds) and priorities. If clients have needs which do not fall within these criteria, they may not be eligible for services. At the same time, the continuing care needs of people discharged from hospital have severely stretched local authority resources, so that in some cases even assessed needs cannot be fully provided for.

Making minor adjustments to eligibility criteria to include or exclude certain types of need is one way that social services departments control spending on community care services. In 1994, for example, Gloucestershire and the Isle of Wight revised their eligibility criteria to limit access to services because community care spending had been higher than anticipated.

It is vital for service users that there is consensus among care management staff about how eligibility criteria are applied, and about how subsequent changes in eligibility are interpreted. Training is often the best way to achieve this. If staff involved in assessment do not have a shared understanding of the eligibility criteria they are using, each person may interpret and apply them differently. This can result in inequalities in who does and does not receive services. You also need to keep yourself informed about available budgets, and to share ideas and information about the full range of available services and creative ways of using them.

CHECK YOUR OWN PRACTICE

- How are eligibility criteria for community care services decided? Do you have any input to this process?
- Have staff who do assessments received training or reached a consensus about how eligibility criteria are interpreted and applied?
- Are you well informed about all the budgets available to you, and what they can be used for?

- Do you make full use of the budgets/resources that are available, or are you under pressure to spend less?

- How do you know that you are getting the most for the individual client out of available budgets? Could you get more, without reducing quality, by doing things in a different way?

Making the most of available budgets is an important part of care management; this and other financial skills are explored in Chapter 7. Service development officers, the budget-holder to whom you are responsible, and the community care finance section or officer are likely to be useful sources of information.

The shift from free health care towards means-tested social care

The development of community care services means that hospital patients who need continuing care are often discharged much earlier than they used to be. This has been matched by a substantial reduction in the number of long-stay hospital beds. Because patients go either to their own home and the care of their family or to a care home, the costs of continuing care for health authorities are reduced. Some of the costs of care have transferred to social services departments, who meet the costs of needs assessment and – for users who cannot afford to pay – the costs of residential home care and in some cases of nursing home care. Some costs have transferred to the relatives or friends who become carers. Many carers give up work, thus losing income and in the longer term National Insurance benefits and pension rights. Collectively, unpaid carers save the Treasury millions of pounds every year.

Some costs have transferred to service users. NHS health care is generally free to service users, but social services departments are expected to charge those service users who can afford to pay. Users are means-tested and charged according to their ability to pay. Government funding for social care is at present based on the expectation that local authorities will raise 9 per cent of the funds they need for domiciliary and day care services from charges to service users. Community care plans (see p 32) must contain details of charging policies and arrangements for financial assessment.

Community care manager: 'The assessment process is not what it should be. It is supposed to identify clients' needs and preferences but it is really about assessing what proportion of State funding the client should receive.'

Practitioners involved in assessment and care planning are likely to find themselves negotiating with NHS colleagues in the grey and frequently disputed area between NHS and local authority responsibility for continuing care needs. Care management staff are at the sharp end of administering the shift in the costs of care. They are also at the sharp end of explaining to clients that some of the costs have shifted to them.

Local policies and procedures for the financial administration of community care services vary widely. You need to be well informed about them, and ensure that service users are also fully informed as part of the assessment and care planning process.

CHECK YOUR OWN PRACTICE

- Do you fully understand local policies for financing health and social care?

- Do you understand the policies surrounding the choices (or lack of choices) available to clients for residential/nursing home care or care at home?

- Can you explain policies and the choices they permit to clients in terms that they will understand?

- Do you make sure clients and carers fully understand the costs to them of different options for care?

- Do you understand the financial assessment process, and take care to explain it fully to clients – or at least know what sources of advice you can draw on?

Advocacy or managing the budget?

Advocacy is an integral part of care management, in that your role is to interpret the client's needs and wishes and to translate these into the individual care requirements that you specify to the provider. You may also have to argue for your client's interests within your own organisation (for example with the budget-holder) or with other professionals or agencies.

There must also be limits to advocacy as part of the care management role, and you should be clear about these. Your role as a purchaser may at times be in conflict with the needs of your client. For example, if you control your own budget and a service user wants to appeal against a decision relating to the assessment or care plan, or wants to know how to reduce or minimise the charges they will pay, you should recognise that this calls for independent advocacy or advice.

You need to be well informed about health and social services complaints procedures and local sources of independent advice and representation, and be ready to direct clients to an appropriate person or agency.

CHECK YOUR OWN PRACTICE

- If you are responsible for managing or remaining within a budget, can you act as an advocate for clients without any conflict of interest?

- If clients ask you for advice about their finances, or getting access to services, are you clear about the limits of the support you can offer?

- How do you make sure that clients are well informed about procedures for appealing against decisions, making a complaint, asking for a review of services, and getting access to independent advocacy?

We have now looked at the role of care management within the Government's overall policy framework for reforming community care. The Government's approach is only one of a number of possible ways of organising and paying for community care. In time, the lessons learned from implementing this framework will inform new policy and new organisational changes.

In the meantime, the present changes are far-reaching. Not everyone agrees with every part of them, but it is important that everyone involved in care management understands the skills and processes involved in buying care for individual users and, as far as possible, can make the present system work in the best interests of clients.

In Chapter 2 we look at how social services departments purchase community care for their local populations and at the role of care management within this local framework.

RECOMMENDED READING

- *Care Management and Assessment: Managers' Guide* (1991) Department of Health Social Services Inspectorate, Scottish Office Social Work Services Group, HMSO. Official guidance for social services department managers.

- *Care Management and Assessment: Practitioners' Guide* (1991) Department of Health Social Services Inspectorate, Scottish Office Social Work Services Group, HMSO. Official guidance for practitioners.

- 'Care Management around the World' (1995) David Challis, in *Care Plan*, June 1995. A review of developments in care management in different countries, and emerging issues and questions for care management in the UK.

- *The Community Care Handbook: The reformed system explained* (1995) Barbara Meredith, ACE Books. This provides a comprehensive overview of community care reforms, explains their varied implementation, and discusses how the system has evolved.

- *Social Work and Community Care* (1995) Malcolm Payne, Macmillan. Chapter 2 'The development of community care in the social services' and Chapter 3 'Care management and social work' provide a useful critical review of the history of community care policy and care management.

Other official guidance referred to in this chapter

- *Community Care: Agenda for action. A report to the Secretary of State for Social Services* (1988) HMSO (Griffiths report).

- *Caring for People: Community care in the next decade and beyond* (1989) Cm 849, HMSO (White Paper).

- *Community Care in the Next Decade and Beyond: Policy Guidance* (1990) HMSO.

2 How local authorities purchase care

The aim of this chapter is to describe how care management fits into the overall purchase of care by social services departments. It explains Government guidance on purchasing care and looks at how local authorities have developed their purchasing role. It describes how care management fits into this role, and explains the relationship between buying care for individual clients and purchasing services for the local population.

QUESTIONS THIS CHAPTER WILL TRY TO ANSWER

- How does the care you buy fit into the local authority's overall plans for community care services?

- What systems and procedures have social services departments developed for planning and purchasing care services?

- How does care management fit in with purchasing at the strategic level?

REFORMED FUNCTIONS OF SOCIAL SERVICES DEPARTMENTS

Since 1993, all local authorities have been required to:

- prepare community care plans which state the objectives, priorities and targets of community care, and identify how the local authority will encourage independent sector provision of services – these plans must be made public;

- assess individuals' needs for community care services;

- buy care from the independent sector: 85 per cent of the transfer element of the Special Transitional Grant was to be spent in the independent sector (see pp 22–23);
- monitor all aspects of community care plans and feed this information into an annual review;
- establish inspection units to inspect all residential homes in the area, including those run by the social services department (nursing homes are registered and inspected by health authorities under separate regulations);
- provide information to the public about service provision.

The purchase of care is intended to be part of a circular process, in which information from needs assessment and care management is fed into the planning process. This in turn helps to shape future commissioning and purchasing. The diagram overleaf shows how this should happen.

The objectives and priorities of your social services department's current community care plan should have some bearing on the objectives and priorities of front-line workers, and there should be channels for care management staff to feed back information into the planning process. In practice, systems to enable this cycle of planning, purchasing, provision and review have been slow to develop.

Social worker: 'The community care plan? It's a bit of an enigma. I saw a copy once, but it has never been suggested to our team that it has any relevance to our work.'

HOW LOCAL AUTHORITIES HAVE DEVELOPED THEIR PURCHASING ROLE

Government reforms aimed to change social services departments from direct providers of community care services to enabling authorities – that is, planners and purchasers of care services. A key element in this change is the separation between purchaser and provider roles. The underlying aim is to transfer the provision of a substantial volume of services from the public sector to the independent sector (private, not-for-profit and voluntary organisations). This transfer has met with differing degrees of

MANAGING CARE IN THE COMMUNITY

Users and carers should be involved at every stage of the planning cycle, at strategic level through representative bodies such as users' and carers' groups, and at care management level through close consultation with the individual needing care.

Other pressures for change
National, regional and local policy
Local demands
Available resources

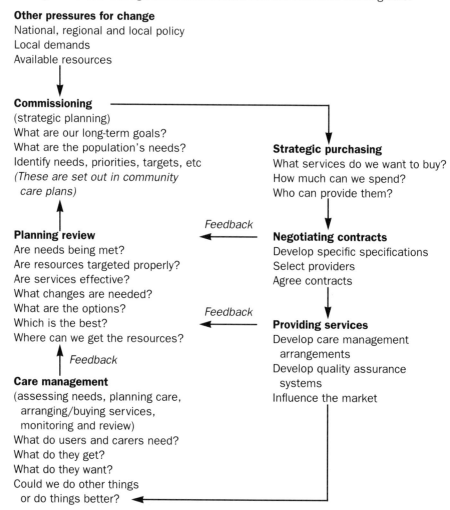

Commissioning
(strategic planning)
What are our long-term goals?
What are the population's needs?
Identify needs, priorities, targets, etc
*(These are set out in community
care plans)*

Planning review
Are needs being met?
Are resources targeted properly?
Are services effective?
What changes are needed?
What are the options?
Which is the best?
Where can we get the resources?

Feedback

Care management
(assessing needs, planning care,
arranging/buying services,
monitoring and review)
What do users and carers need?
What do they get?
What do they want?
Could we do other things
or do things better?

Strategic purchasing
What services do we want to buy?
How much can we spend?
Who can provide them?

Feedback

Negotiating contracts
Develop specific specifications
Select providers
Agree contracts

Feedback

Providing services
Develop care management
arrangements
Develop quality assurance
systems
Influence the market

Source Adapted from N Yorks Community Care Plan, County Module, 1994–95, p 25.

compliance and opposition, sometimes depending on the political complexion of individual local authorities. As a result there is considerable variation in the purchasing arrangements of different authorities. The following sections describe in general terms how social services departments have developed their purchasing role, but you also need to understand how this happens in practice in your own authority. The questions are designed to help you do this.

Becoming enabling authorities has involved social services departments in major organisational changes and new activities. The key ones are:

- separating purchasing and providing functions;
- developing care management and assessment;
- deciding how far to delegate (devolve) budgets;
- developing financial management systems;
- developing contracts;
- planning and managing the 'social care market';
- developing joint planning and commissioning with health authorities.

SEPARATING PURCHASING AND PROVIDING FUNCTIONS

Government guidance on the purchase of services defines purchasing as 'the assessment of individuals' need, the arrangements and purchase of service to meet them'. This is not the same as directly providing services. Some social services departments have fully separated the management of purchasing and providing, from senior management level downwards. An example of this is illustrated in the diagram overleaf.

Some departments have separated the management of purchasing and providing at a lower level within the department; this might happen, for example, at the level of client groups or geographical areas. The diagram overleaf shows an example.

The way that local authorities separate purchasing and providing roles may vary between client groups or between geographical areas, or it may follow the historical pattern of existing services. Some local authorities have tried to avoid the purchaser–provider separation as far as possible,

FULL SEPARATION OF PURCHASING AND PROVIDING ROLES

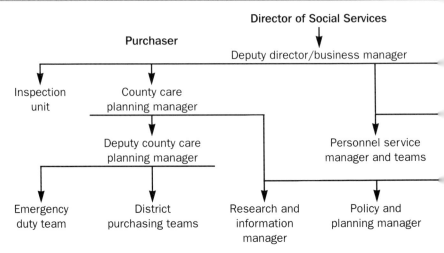

Source *GNVQ Advanced Health and Social Care* (1995) Liam Clarke et al, Stanley Thornes, p 266.

SEPARATION OF PURCHASING AND PROVIDING ROLES AT A LOWER LEVEL

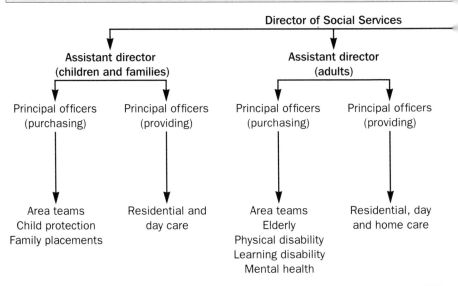

Source *Intermediate Health and Social Care GNVQ* (1995) Neil Moonie (ed), Heinemann, p 139.

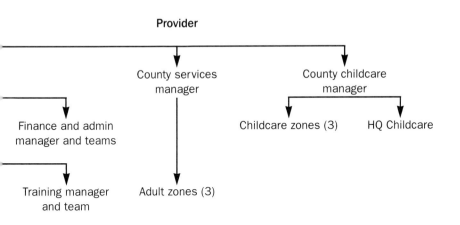

Provider

County services manager

County childcare manager

Finance and admin manager and teams

Childcare zones (3)

HQ Childcare

Training manager and team

Adult zones (3)

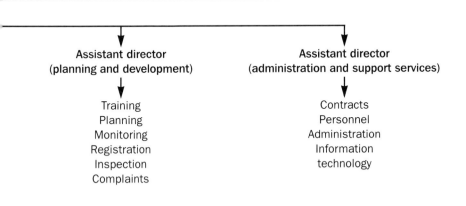

Assistant director (planning and development)

Assistant director (administration and support services)

Training
Planning
Monitoring
Registration
Inspection
Complaints

Contracts
Personnel
Administration
Information
technology

because they are opposed to the Government's aim of reducing public provision of services.

Different ways of separating purchasing and providing have their own advantages and disadvantages. Whatever the structure, a good deal of its strength will depend on how well it is managed and how good the flow of information is. Information needs to move efficiently between people working at the same level and from front-line workers upwards, as well as from senior management downwards.

An awareness of the differences in the way social services departments organise their purchasing and providing roles is helpful if you deal with colleagues from other authorities, or if you move to a job in another area.

CHECK THE LOCAL AUTHORITY'S PRACTICE

- Have you read and understood your local authority's community care plans?
- How are purchasing and provision separated in your social services department?

DEVELOPING CARE MANAGEMENT AND ASSESSMENT

Care management refers to any method of identifying and assessing individuals and linking this to the arrangement and monitoring of services to the individual in a systematic way. There are different approaches to care management; the tasks described on page 24 may be performed by a single worker or shared between several people.

Government sees care management as central to the development of the care market, which it believes to be the most efficient way of providing services. Because care management staff assess and arrange services, they potentially act as 'brokers' (matching services to needs) for the whole range of public and independent services. Government guidance on purchasing issued in 1991 envisaged that the purchaser–provider separation would work best 'when purchasing power is close to the client' – that is, when care management staff have budgetary control and can buy the most suitable services for their client from a range of providers.

The functions of care management

Government guidance suggests that a good care management system has several functions.

Care management should help target resources efficiently

Care management can be used as a mechanism which enables SSDs to target scarce resources on those with greatest need, and this suggests a system of screening. It implies the concentration of resources primarily on individuals on the margins of residential care with a view to substituting intensive domiciliary and day care where this is considered appropriate.

Purchase of Service, para 2.3.5

The phrase 'target resources on those with greatest need' refers to a way of achieving efficiency in the use of resources, but it also implies the exclusion of those with lesser needs. The Government wishes to see a move from *universal* provision to *selective* provision. A key part of the care management worker's new role is therefore to ration resources through the mechanism of assessment.

Feedback from care management should inform the planning process

If services are targeted and responsive to need, information systems must enable feedback from care management about service shortfall and user preferences to be fed into service planning and review. The feedback is part of the planning cycle illustrated on p 34, and should be combined with feedback from service users, carers and providers and the views of the local community. At present, because of concerns about legal action if there is shown to be a shortfall in services, this feedback loop is not well developed in all local authorities. (For more information about systems for recording unmet need, see pp 59–61. Monitoring and review in care management should ideally be part of a wider social services quality assurance system – see 'Care management and quality', pp 113–115.)

Care management should focus on purchasing rather than providing services

Although assessing need and arranging services has to some extent always been a part of social work practice, care management represents an important shift away from the traditional pattern of social work, which generally involved some direct provision of therapeutic care or support (for example, enabling, supporting and protecting clients and families through counselling, mediation and advocacy). The emphasis in care management is on purchasing, not provision. In practice, some social services departments have developed the purchasing aspect of the care management worker's role more than others. In a number of authorities, front-line workers are under pressure to draw on local authority services first, only purchasing from external providers when no directly provided service is available. One advantage of separating purchasing and providing is that, in principle, there is no conflict of interest between purchasing and provision for a front-line worker who does not have a provider role. In addition, with a care manager coordinating services, their delivery should be less fragmented. The disadvantage may in some cases be a greater lack of continuity of care: at times, clients receiving care services from several different providers feel that the care delivered is fragmented and disorganised.

THE RELATIONSHIP BETWEEN SOCIAL WORK AND CARE MANAGEMENT

Social work skills and activities	Care management	Business/admin skills and activities
Interpersonal skills	Assessment	Managing budgets
Counselling	Care planning	Sourcing suppliers
Group work	Arranging/buying care services	Costing care plans
Empowering clients		Dealing with contracts
Promoting self-determination	Monitoring	
	Review	Negotiating prices
Developing community resources		Monitoring quality of supply
Promoting equality of opportunity and access		Managing information
		Compiling records
		Processing invoices
Multi-disciplinary working		Inter-agency coordination

This diagram shows some of the key social work and business/administrative skills used in care management. The skills drawn on and the way they are combined vary widely in different authorities.

Care management should promote individual choice and self-determination

One of the objectives of care management is to promote individual choice and self-determination (*Policy Guidance*, para 3.3). A Direction from the Secretary of State for Health (known as the Direction on Choice) requires local authorities to arrange a place in a care home of a person's choice, provided that certain conditions are met. The way in which the Direction is interpreted varies between authorities, but in many areas it has meant that people needing a home are now offered fuller information and a wider choice of options. (Circular LAC(92)27 *The National Assistance Act 1948 (Choice of Accommodation) Directions* and Circular LAC(93)18 *The National Assistance Act 1948 (Choice of Accommodation) (Amendment) Directions.*) The Direction does not at present extend to domiciliary care, and there is not yet the same degree of choice available for domiciliary service users.

Ensuring that users and carers have access to representation or advocacy, or someone to interpret for them, is an important way of promoting choice. Government guidance asks local authorities to make arrangements to promote self-advocacy or to ensure access to independent advocacy services for users who cannot represent themselves (*Care Management and Assessment: Managers' Guide*, paras 2.43–2.53). You need to be well informed about your local authority's arrangements to promote self-advocacy and advocacy schemes, and about local guidance on which clients are eligible for referral to advocacy or interpreting services in what circumstances.

CHECK THE LOCAL AUTHORITY'S PRACTICE

- How does your department monitor unmet need?
- How does the care management approach adopted in your local authority compare with the objectives described in this section?

DEVELOPING FINANCIAL MANAGEMENT SYSTEMS

Social services departments need adequate financial management systems if they are to meet Government's policy objectives. Financial management systems need to take account of purchasing at senior management level (buying a block of services) and at care management level (buying services for individual clients). This means that senior managers have to:

- decide overall budgets, priorities and eligibility criteria for services;

- decide who will be budget-holders and to what level to devolve decisions;

- monitor outcomes (ie the results of providing a service) and use information about identified shortfalls in services in future budget planning.

The development of financial management systems creates three major areas of responsibility for staff with a care management role, whether or not they are budget-holders:

To the social services department – to remain within available budgets, and to keep an accurate record of any transactions that they agree. Budget-holders, planners and purchasers also need information about how care management staff are currently purchasing services in order to make future decisions.

To individual clients – to arrange or buy the best quality care within available budgets.

To service providers – to supply them with information so that they can do their job properly, with effective contracts, and to make sure that they receive prompt payment.

Most local authorities have developed or are developing computerised information systems for financial management; this is one of the reasons for the extra paperwork (and/or computer skills) that front-line workers have had to get to grips with since the community care reforms.

CHECK YOUR OWN PRACTICE

- How good is your understanding of your own department's financial management systems?

- Do you know why you are asked for the information that you provide, and how it is processed and used?

- How much time and priority should you give to paperwork for financial management and administration?

Some of these questions are discussed in Chapter 7. If you would like to know more about your social services department's financial systems, the information manager, the relevant finance officer or your budget-holder may be able to help.

DEVOLVING BUDGETS

Government wants to see social services budgets delegated to the staff who assess needs and arrange care for individuals. Where the supply of services is decided centrally, it is the Government's view that social services departments tend to be over-concerned with the take-up of existing services. Devolving budgets to care management staff is seen as an effective way of changing this historical pattern of service provision (*Purchase of Service*, para 2.4.5).

This parallels Government policy of delegating or devolving budgets in other public sector services over the last 15 years. It has happened in education with the local management of schools (where school governors are responsible for the budget), and in the NHS with the setting up of NHS trusts (whose trustees are responsible for the budget) and the introduction of GP fundholding (where GPs manage their own budgets).

Government policy in this area reflects the management technique of dividing an organisation into cost centres (ie departments, units or teams with their own budgets) which are responsible for accurately identifying their own costs. This enables management to achieve tighter and more accurate control of overall expenditure within the organisation.

In practice, few local authorities have yet devolved budgets right down to the level of care management staff. Some have resisted this move for political reasons. Some social services departments have moved only very cautiously in this direction, because delegating budgets makes strategic planning more difficult.

CHECK YOUR OWN PRACTICE

- How far have budgets been devolved in your department over the last few years? Are they likely to be devolved further?
- Has devolution of budgets required you to develop new skills?
- Do you feel you have received adequate training in this area?

The level of financial skills that you need will depend to some extent on how far budgets have been or will be devolved in your department. Talk to your line manager or budget-holder for more information. Specific skills are discussed in Chapter 7.

DEVELOPING CONTRACTS

The contract is the tool that the social services department uses to purchase care from external providers. Contracting involves selecting a provider and negotiating an agreement about the services they will provide in return for payment. Social services departments have evolved their own systems for developing and managing contracts, but the following activities are generally carried out by senior management:

- identifying and developing a specification for the service required;
- selecting providers;
- agreeing the awarding of a contract;
- monitoring the contract;
- reviewing contract performance.

Sometimes development work is needed to encourage potential providers, perhaps because none exists in the geographical area for which the service is required or because the authority has identified a need for a new service. This work may be done by the department's service development officers or contracts manager, or by a team of managers. In some cases, development work is undertaken in partnership with a provider or group of providers. In some cases, it may be a provider of specialised services who undertakes the development work themselves.

Front-line workers with a care management role are not generally involved in developing service specifications or in negotiating with potential providers to establish a new service, though you may be asked to comment on what services are needed or to provide feedback on how services are working. In authorities which have established local purchasing panels or teams, a care management worker may be one of a range of people who provide information for or sit on these panels.

How far those involved in care management have responsibility for selecting providers and agreeing contracts depends on the way in which the authority organises its strategic purchasing. Some authorities have developed lists of approved providers who have agreed to meet certain quality standards, and front-line workers select from this approved list. Most authorities have standardised service specifications and contracts, so that the front-line worker negotiates only the details of the individual service to be provided to the client, based on the care plan.

Whatever freedom you have in selecting providers and whatever scope you have to negotiate the details of the care plan with providers, the way that you carry out these activities should be based on sound principles and a clear understanding of the purpose of the contract. These issues are discussed in Chapters 4 and 5. The contracts manager will be a good source of information about your own authority's systems for purchasing and contracting.

JOINT WORKING WITH HEALTH AUTHORITIES

Joint working with health authorities is central to social services departments' enabling and purchasing role. Joint working arrangements are not new, but the Government wishes to see more extensive collaboration in the planning of community care services, the provision of services and the purchasing of services from other public and independent providers (*Purchase of Service*, para 2.4.11).

At the strategic level, joint working enables health and local authorities to develop complementary or shared plans, to agree priorities and responsibilities, and to avoid duplication or gaps in services. At the operational level, health and local authorities have to agree how workers from each organisation are to collaborate in care management and assessment arrangements for clients with complex needs.

District Health Authorities were required to separate purchasing and providing in 1991. Since then District Health Authorities and Family Health Services Authorities have merged, and the number of NHS trusts and GP fundholders has increased, so that the organisation and funding of local health services has become quite complex. Some knowledge of these structures, and of how health authorities purchase care, can help you to understand the constraints within which health service colleagues are working.

The withdrawal of hospital beds for patients who need long-term or continuing care has increased the number of people being discharged from hospital with overlapping health and social care needs. You may be responsible, in collaboration with health professionals, for planning care for this grey area of need. You may be aware that the question of who funds the provision has been a source of dispute between health and local authorities. The Government asked health authorities to consult locally and produce their own criteria for funding people with continuing care needs by April 1996. In Chapter 1 we emphasised the need for a shared understanding of social services eligibility criteria, to ensure that they are not applied differently by different care management workers. You also need to be sure that you and colleagues with whom you collaborate have a shared understanding of health authority eligibility criteria.

CHECK YOUR OWN PRACTICE

- Do you understand the management and funding framework of the health services with which you work?
- Do you, other care management staff, and health service colleagues involved in assessment and care planning have a shared understanding of health authority criteria for funding people with continuing care needs?

PLANNING AND MANAGING THE 'SOCIAL CARE MARKET'

The Government wishes to create a market for social care (see p 11 on terminology). This requires suppliers and purchasers. Social services departments have considerable purchasing power; to bring new suppliers, or providers, into the market, the Government required social services departments to spend a substantial proportion of the Special Transitional Grant in the independent sector. The Government expects social services departments to use their commercial power to plan and shape the development of local markets (*Purchase of Service*, para 2.1.13).

Local authorities vary in the way they have chosen to develop the local pattern of suppliers. Some have sought to maintain their own directly provided services as far as possible and to purchase only services which complement these or fill gaps in provision; some have enabled directly provided services to become independent 'not-for-profit' organisations. Some authorities have developed at least some services with independent providers on a partnership basis while others award most contracts by a process of tender. Some authorities have actively helped voluntary organisations to develop as independent providers; in other areas support for the voluntary sector has been less forthcoming. Some authorities have reduced their directly provided services to a minimum and opted for an open market, encouraging competition between a large number of independent providers.

Most front-line workers involved in care management have some flexibility in selecting providers. You should be aware that your own actions also shape the market. Demand produces supply, and where you place demand will shape the pattern of future supply.

Buying from a single provider could lead to that supplier having a monopoly and charging unrealistic prices for an indifferent service. On the other hand, buying from a wide range of suppliers could lead to uncertainties in supply, variation in quality and high monitoring costs. Certain services must be provided by law. This may influence the way in which the local authority decides to arrange or purchase them, and from whom they purchase them.

CHECK YOUR OWN PRACTICE

- How well do you understand your role in shaping the market?
- How do you make decisions about what services to buy from which providers?
- What guidance are you given, if any, by your line manager/budget-holder?
- How do your decisions affect the pattern of supply?

BUYING FROM MONOPOLY AND MULTIPLE SUPPLIERS: ADVANTAGES AND DISADVANTAGES

Monopoly supplier	Multiple suppliers
Without competition, may charge high prices	*Competition between suppliers helps to keep prices down*
May become complacent about service quality. Having only one supplier may result in a lack of choice for service users	*Competition may increase suppliers' readiness to be responsive and flexible*
May be known to supply a service to consistently satisfactory standards	*Wide range of standards of service: standards may be less known or untested*
Quicker to deal with one large supplier	*More administration time and paperwork needed to deal with several suppliers*
May be known to be reliable, therefore requires less monitoring	*More time needed to monitor reliability, quality, etc, because there are several suppliers*
Assured demand may enable supplier to maintain training, pay levels, motivated staff, quality of care	*Unpredictable demand may make it difficult to maintain quality of staff and service*
Larger supplier may have enough flexibility to ensure availability, even when demand fluctuates	*Availability of service may fluctuate*

CHECK YOUR OWN PRACTICE

- Selecting suppliers and negotiating the care plan takes time. Do you cost the time you spend in dealing with providers?

- Are you investing time to develop an adequate future supply of services, to ensure quality and to negotiate the right price?

- Do you waste time chasing or checking up on providers who are disorganised, inefficient or providing poor-quality care?

Social services departments are developing quality assurance systems to help ensure that care management time is not spent on sorting out other agencies' inefficiencies – see Chapter 6.

We have now looked at the relationship between care management and local authority purchasing strategy. In the next chapter we will discuss the relationship between care management and service users.

RECOMMENDED READING

- *Caring for People: Purchase of Service, Practice Guidance and practice material for social services departments and other agencies* (1991) Department of Health Social Services Inspectorate, HMSO. Chapter 2 'The mixed economy of care' sets out how local authorities should develop arrangements for strategic purchasing and care management.

- *Purchasing for Health* (1995) John Øvretveit, Open University Press. Chapter 8 'Collaboration with local authorities', written from a health service viewpoint, discusses the purpose of collaboration between health authorities and local authorities, the joint tasks that can be carried out at different levels of the organisations, and the advantages and disadvantages of joint working.

  Other official guidance referred to in this chapter
- *Care Management and Assessment: Managers' Guide* (1991) Department of Health Social Services Inspectorate, Scottish Office Social Work Services Group, HMSO. Official guidance for social services department managers.

- Circular LAC(92)27 *The National Assistance Act 1948 (Choice of Accommodation) Directions* (1992) Department of Health.

- Circular LAC(93)18 *The National Assistance Act 1948 (Choice of Accommodation) (Amendment) Directions* (1993) Department of Health.

- *Community Care in the Next Decade and Beyond: Policy Guidance* (1990) HMSO.

3 Buying care to meet users' needs

This chapter looks at the objectives of care management and the tasks involved, and reviews the skills needed to buy care to meet users' needs. It provides an extended checklist to help you think about the business side of care management arrangements in your own organisation, and the skills you need in your own practice. Each section tells you where you can find more information about a particular topic in later chapters.

QUESTIONS THIS CHAPTER WILL TRY TO ANSWER

- What is the purpose of care management?
- What are the practical, financial and administrative skills needed to deal with the business side of care management?
- How do we know whether care management is effective?

THE OBJECTIVES OF CARE MANAGEMENT

The broad purpose of care management is to tailor services to meet users' assessed needs. Front-line workers and their managers need to be clear about the specific objectives of care management in order to know what they are aiming for and how to assess their progress.

Although local authorities are developing widely differing ways of organising care management tasks, different systems are working towards the same objectives:

- to ensure that the resources available are used in the most effective way to meet individual care needs;

- to restore and maintain independence by enabling people to live in the community wherever possible;

- to work to prevent or to minimise the effects of disability and illness in people of all ages;

- to treat those who need services with respect and provide equal opportunities for all;

- to promote individual choice and self-determination, and build on existing strengths and care resources;

- to promote partnership between users, carers and service providers in all sectors, together with organisations of and for each group. (*Policy Guidance*, para 3.3)

The central point is that care management is about balancing differing and sometimes conflicting goals. This involves different kinds of activities, and gives rise to tensions which you need to be aware of and find ways of working with.

QUALITY ASSURANCE IN CARE MANAGEMENT

Quality assurance is a way of checking whether care management arrangements are achieving their objectives. A quality assurance system encourages managers and front-line workers to ask the questions below, and looks for ways of answering them:

- What is the purpose of care management?
- How do we balance the different elements in care management?
- How can we measure care management? What results do we want? How do we know if we are being effective?

Government guidance says that there should be clear standards of practice and monitoring mechanisms to ensure that staff with care management responsibilities are providing an effective service. Standards include things like response times, sharing of information, user and carer involvement, open recording, and decision-making based on clear criteria. Feedback from users and carers on their experience of care management is also a way of measuring quality (*Managers' Guide*, para 3.25).

Government guidance also says that monitoring the quality of services provided to users is a central task of care management: 'Care management should be continually sensitising the agency to issues of quality, both at the level of individual users and at service level reviews.'

Chapter 6 discusses how to promote quality in care management and in the services arranged for clients.

In the following sections we look at the tasks which make up care management, and review the skills and processes needed to perform them effectively. Chapters 4 to 8 will look at the key topics introduced here in more detail; working through this review may be useful in deciding which topics you want to concentrate on.

ARRANGING THE ASSESSMENT

Local authorities have different procedures for deciding what level of assessment is needed and who should do it. Most social services departments have developed and adapted their assessment procedures over time, as staff identify ways of making them more effective. The checklist below sets out some helpful principles that can apply to all assessments, although they may need adapting to suit local procedures.

CHECKLIST: GIVING USERS INFORMATION ABOUT THE ASSESSMENT

- When you first make contact to arrange the assessment, do you always allow enough time to explain what assessment involves and to allow the client to ask questions?

- Do you check out the client's communication needs? If someone has difficulty in being understood, what support do you need to arrange? Do they need an interpreter or an advocate? It is not good practice to carry out an assessment if you have not arranged proper support to enable the client to communicate with you.

- Do you check that clients are well informed beforehand about the assessment and the care management process? Do you send written information or give it verbally? What about clients who have difficulty with communication? Information empowers users, and they cannot contribute fully to the assessment or make informed decisions without it.

- Would it be useful to suggest that the user or carer keeps a diary until the assessment takes place, where this is appropriate, with details of their day-to-day routine, current difficulties, and solutions or support that would help them? Explain that this is to help you get a detailed picture, but be careful not to raise false expectations.

- Do you make clear to clients how long the assessment is likely to take? Find out if they will be able to sit through a long discussion, if there are good and bad times of day for them, and if they need to make special arrangements.

- Do you explain what kind of questions you will ask, and make sure clients will have privacy if they do not wish to answer very personal questions in front of someone else?

- Do you check arrangements for interviewing the carer? Will the carer be present at the assessment? Does the user want the carer to be present throughout? Do you arrange to interview the carer alone?

CARRYING OUT THE ASSESSMENT

Assessment procedures vary to match users' circumstances and complexity of needs, but the aim of assessment is to give users and carers an opportunity to discuss their needs and difficulties, to discover their strengths and to explore possible solutions.

The assessment form should be a tool which enables you to gather together different types of information to build up a broad picture. It should not be used simply to record information about the person's illness or disability.

Some assessment procedures tend to focus on the user's readiness to move to other accommodation (eg from hospital to a care home) or their suitability for a particular type of accommodation or service rather than finding out about their potential capabilities and aspirations.

A needs-led assessment depends on obtaining good-quality information from the user and carer. The assessment form is the means by which you record information, and it should be designed to do this well. It should help you to discuss with the user and clearly record their view of their needs, wants and preferences. It should also enable you to explore future possibilities with the user in an open-ended way.

CHECK YOUR OWN PRACTICE

■ How comprehensive is the information you record?

■ Does the assessment explore the individual's potential capabilities, preferences and aspirations, or does it simply concentrate on one dimension such as:
  – difficulties or disabilities?
  – readiness to move?
  – suitability for a service?

Accommodation

For many elderly and disabled people, the layout and physical condition of their home can cause major difficulties (cold, damp, draughts, disrepair; difficult access to toilet, bath, kitchen, etc). Assessment procedures do not always give users and carers enough time or space to discuss their concerns about their living conditions. Making time to discuss equipment, adaptations or structural changes may suggest solutions that will enable the user to continue living at home, or perhaps reduce the user's need to rely on other forms of support.

CHECK YOUR OWN PRACTICE

■ What space do you give in assessment to discussing the user's home environment?

Social networks

The service user's social networks – family, friends, neighbours, church, clubs, workmates or former workmates – may be an important source of informal support, or of potential support which you may be able to develop or formalise. The assessment process should help you to identify strengths in the user's existing network and possibilities for future development. It should also enable you to identify the user's social needs and aspirations (for example, to have company at home, visit a relative, go to the pub, pursue a hobby). Keeping a diary can help you and the service user to begin mapping social networks.

CHECK YOUR OWN PRACTICE

- How do you identify resources in your client's existing social network?
- How do you identify your client's social needs and aspirations?

Risk assessment

The person being assessed may prefer to accept certain risks which their relatives or neighbours feel are unacceptable. A frail elderly person may, for example, insist that he or she would rather accept the risk of another fall at home than the alternative of residential care. The aim of assessment is to minimise risk by providing services, equipment or training. In this case grab rails and a personal alarm might help to reduce the risk of serious harm from a fall.

As with any aspect of care management, assessment of risk should be done in a consistent way. As far as possible, clients facing similar risks should be offered the same degree of choice, whoever carries out the assessment. Some agencies have developed clear guidelines and risk assessment tools to try to make this process as consistent as possible. In other agencies, more decisions are left to the professional judgement of the person doing the assessment.

Another area of risk is that of abuse from a carer. You should be thoroughly familiar with your social services department's policy and procedure in this area. In some cases, it may be important to assess the person needing care on their own and to talk to the carer separately. If you suspect there may be abuse, get advice from your line manager immediately.

CHECK YOUR OWN PRACTICE

- Does the assessment procedure enable you to discuss fully risks to the user or others and weigh these up against the user's right to independence and choice?
- Do you have a good working knowledge of:
  - local policy or guidance on risk assessment?
  - legislation and guidance on moving and handling?

Carer's assessment

The Carers Act 1995, implemented in April 1996, gives 'those providing or intending to provide substantial and regular care' the right to a carer's assessment when the person they are caring for is assessed or reassessed. At present, draft Government guidance says that the assessment should cover the carer's perception of the situation, tasks undertaken, tasks the carer would like help with, and the carer's emotional, mental and physical health.

Carers may want support to continue caring or they may want to explore alternatives because they are no longer able or willing to care. Your role in the assessment may be to help the user and carer discuss their conflicting needs and to negotiate a solution which is as far as possible acceptable to both of them.

CHECK YOUR OWN PRACTICE

- How do you assess the needs of the carer?
- What do you do when the carer's needs or wishes conflict with those of the user?

Bringing in other professionals

The Government wishes to see closer coordination of multidisciplinary working. Where a person has housing or health care needs as well as social care needs, or complex social care needs requiring specialised care, you will need to involve other professionals in assessment and care planning. You should as far as possible obtain the user's permission to do this. You should also be clear about policy and guidance on when and how to involve other people from within your own agency (for example your line manager or an occupational therapist), or from other agencies (for example a community nurse, housing officer or speech therapist). It is important that there is consistency in the way care management staff use other professional resources in assessment: this is another area which requires a clear shared understanding of roles and resources, and well-developed channels of communication.

CHECK YOUR OWN PRACTICE

- Do you always ask for the user's consent before involving other professionals or giving them personal information?
- Are you clear about who to involve and when?

Financial assessment

The purpose of the financial assessment is to determine how much the user will contribute to the cost of services provided. This involves asking for information about current income and expenditure, savings, pensions, insurance policies, and so on. Users often find these questions intrusive, and many people do not welcome the idea that they may have to contribute towards the cost of services they are offered. Administering the financial assessment can be complicated, especially if the user's finances are complex, and many front-line workers do not like doing it.

Financial assessment is not simply about recording details of the user's assets and income. You also have a responsibility to make sure that users are getting all the financial help they are entitled to, and that you get a full picture of what they spend each week. An illness or disability almost always involves extra expenses, which people may forget to mention unless you specifically ask.

People who need community care services are often living in poverty; helping users to make the most of their own resources is therefore an essential part of effective care management. This means being clear about the limits of your own competence to give such advice. One Citizens Advice Bureau (CAB) manager estimates that it takes CAB workers two years to become fully competent in this area. Err on the side of caution and refer users to more specialised sources of help if in doubt. The social services finance department may be a valuable source of information and advice over certain issues.

Some local authorities are looking at formally linking community care assessments with welfare rights and benefits advice, for example by attaching welfare rights workers to community care assessment teams, or making information and discussion about welfare rights an integral part of the assessment process. Keep a list of local agencies such as the CAB and other independent welfare rights schemes who can give advice.

Good practice in financial assessment is discussed in more detail in Chapter 7.

CHECK YOUR OWN PRACTICE

- Do you take care to explain beforehand what financial questions you need to ask, and why, and make sure that clients can give this information in privacy if they wish?

- Does the financial assessment form enable you to explore with clients how they can make most use of their own financial resources?

- Does it enable you to record a detailed picture of expenditure?

- Are you clear about the limits of the advice you are qualified to give users and carers about money matters?

- Are you well informed about local sources of financial advice and how clients can get access to them?

THE CARE PLAN

Developing the care plan may involve negotiation with other professionals, with the budget-holder, and with the user and carer. Care planning should be an opportunity for different workers to exchange ideas and information and discuss what care and support they can provide now and in the future; it is also a time for you to discuss options and preferences with the user. You will need to check that the user understands the likely costs of the available options. The completed care plan should state the objectives or desired outcomes of the action proposed, once these have been discussed and agreed with the user and carer.

The care plan is a specification – that is, it should accurately specify the details of the services to be provided to the user. If difficulties or disagreements arise later about the services that are provided, the care plan should provide an accurate and detailed record of what has been agreed with the user and negotiated with the provider.

WHAT THE CARE PLAN SHOULD CONTAIN

The care plan should set out:

- the objectives or desired outcomes identified by the assessment;
- the components of the care package, and how these link to the outcomes;
- who will provide each component of the package, and when it will start and finish;
- a review date for the care plan;
- the name of the person (eg care manager/key worker) that the user or carer can contact if there are queries or difficulties.

Using the care plan as a specification for individual care is a key skill which is discussed in detail in Chapter 5.

CHECK YOUR OWN PRACTICE

- Do you involve service users as far as possible in developing the care plan?
- Are you able to offer genuine choice to users?
- Do you discuss their preferences for the choices available?
- Do you make sure that users understand the financial implications of different options?
- Does the care plan set out objectives and specify in detail the action agreed?

Recording unmet need

The inevitable consequence of the Government's policy of targeting resources is that in some cases a needs assessment may result in a decision not to provide services. In other cases a lack of resources may mean that the individual's assessed needs cannot be fully met. Such situations are stressful for the practitioner as well as the client. The discussion which follows may help you to identify practical ways in which some of these situations might be changed. Talk to your line manager, other front-line workers and users' groups to explore possibilities. Recording information about unmet need and shortfalls in services is an important part of individual care planning. This feedback is a key element in the cycle of community care planning and purchasing that is described on page 34.

Information about unmet need should be taken into account in future service development and planning.

Systems to record unmet need were at first slow to develop. Local authorities found themselves squeezed between shrinking budgets from central government on the one hand and the withdrawal of health service resources for continuing care on the other. This made it difficult to predict what needs could feasibly be met within available resources. At the same time, local authorities were aware that they might be open to legal challenge from users for failing in their 'duty to care' if care plans recorded assessed needs that could not be met. Local authorities gather **quantitative** or 'aggregated' information about unmet need (statistics about how many users have identified particular needs, how often, etc) but front-line workers may be asked not to record unmet needs on the care plan, or to record them under a different heading, such as 'Outstanding issues'.

If a need is not met because the user and front-line worker do not agree about the care plan, the user has no legal right of appeal but can and should ask for a review of the assessment. This kind of appeal against a decision should be handled through the social services department's complaints procedure. You have a responsibility to make sure that the user is fully informed about the complaints procedure, and has access to an advocate if they need support in putting their viewpoint.

Recording qualitative information about unmet need

Qualitative information about unmet need is as important as statistics. What is the exact nature of the need? Why should it be given a higher priority? Are there ways in which the need could be met at low cost, or even no cost? Front-line workers have a detailed understanding of how service priorities and targets work in practice. It may be clear to you, for example, that current eligibility criteria are creating inequalities in who does and does not receive a service. Policy-makers and planners may be unaware that policies are unfair in practice unless there are channels to feed back this information. You may be able to see possible solutions that would cost little or nothing – a minor adjustment in the rostering of a home care service, for example, might make the service more accessible to more users. This kind of detail needs to be recorded, regularly reviewed and, where possible, acted upon if services are to become genuinely needs-led.

This feedback from care management should be part of the social services department's quality assurance system.

CHECK YOUR OWN PRACTICE

- How do you record information about unmet need? Do you know how the information is used?

- Is there a mechanism to feed back qualitative as well as quantitative information to service planners?

- If a service user or carer feels that their needs have not been met, do you explain the procedure for questioning decisions about the assessment and/or care plan?

ARRANGING THE CARE PACKAGE/ NETWORK OF CARE

Government guidance uses the term 'care package' to describe the network of services and support that may be arranged as a result of assessment (in contrast to the pre-reform approach of assessing clients to fit into existing services). Some social services departments prefer terms such as 'network of care' or 'continuum of care services', because it is felt that care services depend on human qualities and interpersonal relationships that cannot be simply described as goods or packages bought and sold.

One objective of care management is to increase the choice of services offered to users. This cannot happen if care planning does not take into account the user's wishes and preferences. This means that you need to be well informed about the range of resources available in the community, good at thinking creatively, and flexible in your approach to problem-solving.

Sourcing suppliers

'Sourcing' is a business term which means 'identifying sources of supply'. It is a useful term to describe a key difference between traditional social work, which involved coordinating existing services and liaising with other agencies, and care management, which involves actively seeking out potential resources and working out which will provide the best solution for the individual user, within the budget available.

Because local authorities have had to purchase a proportion of services from the independent sector (see pp 22–23), the range of local resources has increased in all parts of the country, though more rapidly in some areas than others. If you are involved in care planning, you must be able to review and update your knowledge of existing and developing providers, and other resources, on a regular basis. You may like to check your own local knowledge using the checklist in Appendix 1.

In some local authorities, information systems to help care management staff to resource care packages/networks have been slow to develop. If you do not have a means of regularly updating your knowledge of available resources, discuss this with your line manager.

CHECK YOUR OWN PRACTICE

- How well informed are you about the range of local resources that you can draw on?

- Do you need to find out more about certain kinds of providers, services or sources of funding?

- How do you get up-to-date information?

Selecting providers

Community care manager: 'When services were all provided in-house, the person who requested a service and the person who arranged its delivery had a mutual understanding of what was needed and how it should be provided. Experience has taught me that you can't take anything for granted with independent providers. Some are very good and very professional, but you can't take things on trust. You have to get everything spelt out to protect yourself and your clients.'

Social welfare officer: 'In the early days we were using the *Yellow Pages* to find domestic cleaning agencies and making arrangements by phone. It wasn't very satisfactory.'

Providers of residential home care must be registered with the social services department and regularly inspected, while **nursing homes** must be registered and inspected by the health authority (dual-registered homes must be registered and inspected by both). This is a way of monitoring the standard of service provided. There is no legal requirement for **providers of domiciliary and day care services** to be registered or inspected, but many local authorities now operate **accreditation** schemes, or lists of **approved providers**; potential providers are then required to demonstrate that they meet certain criteria (for example possession of equipment or facilities, proportion of trained staff, equal opportunities policy) before they are approved.

If your authority does not have a list of approved providers, or if there is no approved provider in your area for a particular service, you may need to investigate and select providers yourself. Your social services department should provide clear guidelines on selecting providers of services for people who are vulnerable, or who would have difficulty communicating their difficulties if they were not receiving a satisfactory service.

Guidelines for minor services (such as a couple of hours domestic cleaning for a physically disabled person) or one-off services (such as intensive cleaning of a house which has been severely neglected) may be quite simple: you may be asked to get three estimates and choose the one which represents best value.

Bear in mind that the best value is not the same as the cheapest, but you may need to argue the case for *not* choosing the cheapest with the budget-holder.

Getting estimates

To compare estimates, you need to be sure that they cover the same service and expenses. Comparing hourly rates for home care services may seem straightforward, but differences in rates may reflect important differences in quality. Rates may be higher because they include expenses (for example travel or equipment) or because the agency uses only experienced or trained staff. Rates may appear lower because there are additional charges which are itemised separately.

- Give as much detail as possible about the service required.
- Ask the agency to give a detailed breakdown of the estimated costs, when relevant, rather than a general figure.

- Always check whether there are additional charges that have not been mentioned, and what they cover. For example, charges for unsocial hours such as weekends and bank holidays can be double the quoted rate.

- Always give a firm deadline for submitting a written estimate – you can waste a great deal of time waiting for or chasing up estimates if you don't give clear deadlines.

Other information to help you compare providers

Estimates cannot really tell you about the quality of service that unknown providers will deliver. To make an informed decision, you need more background information. Below are suggestions about how to obtain this.

Talking to colleagues

Have other colleagues purchased services from the provider? What is their impression of service quality? This kind of information is often available and very useful, but not always shared in an efficient way between staff in different areas, or different parts of the service. If a database or central file to record comments about new providers doesn't exist, consider asking your area manager about starting one.

Meeting the provider

Is it appropriate to meet with the provider or visit the premises? Personal appearances and premises can tell you something about whether the organisation seems efficient and well run. This doesn't necessarily tell you about the quality of service delivered to clients. An unhelpful manager or office which seems badly organised could suggest that the service to clients is also badly run. On the other hand, glossy brochures and high-tech office furniture do not guarantee high standards of care.

Getting a reference

Can the provider give you names of other organisations or individuals who will give a written or telephone reference? It is good practice to ask for some sort of reference, and previous clients do not normally object to being phoned and asked their opinion. If a provider is unwilling to give some sort of reference, this should ring alarm bells. Do not accept general testimonials that cannot be checked.

Is the provider aware of quality issues?

Does the provider belong to a professional association and/or operate a code of practice, set of quality standards, or quality assurance system? None of these is a cast-iron guarantee of quality, but they suggest that the provider is aware of quality issues and may be willing to take positive action if difficulties arise. Some local authorities have encouraged domiciliary care providers to get together and agree their own voluntary code of practice or quality standards. How does the provider handle complaints from clients?

Added value

If there is a significant difference in the estimates you receive, find out why the more expensive suppliers charge more before you reject them. If there is no obvious difference in the service supplied, the cheapest estimate may be the best value. But there are many justifiable reasons for charging more. A supplier's charges may be higher because they:

- train their staff;
- recruit only experienced or trained workers;
- offer a higher level of pay to encourage commitment and stability in their workforce;
- guarantee minimum standards of service;
- demonstrate long-standing expertise and reliability in delivering the service;
- provide continuity of care through the same regular staff.

When charges or estimates are broadly similar, check whether suppliers offer features which represent added value. This can help you decide on the best value, which should be a balance between quality and cost.

Some voluntary organisations offer services with added value. They may charge less than private providers, or provide more for the same price, because they use free volunteer help. Many voluntary organisations recruit and train volunteers with great care, and most volunteers are highly motivated and committed. But the relationship between volunteers, the voluntary organisation and the local authority which contracts for services is a contentious one, as it raises questions about the accountability and possible exploitation of unpaid staff.

The use of volunteers can pose problems if something goes wrong – for example, what if a volunteer sitter fails to turn up when their organisation is under contract to provide a service? The local authority and voluntary organisation need to clarify the role and legal position of volunteers in the contract, and should give clear information to front-line workers, users and volunteers themselves about the scope and limits of volunteers' responsibilities.

Costing the care package

You need to be able to present an accurate calculation of the weekly costs of the care package to your budget-holder. If you are not used to dealing with figures, you may find it complicated to work out the total cost of a range of services, some charged hourly, some weekly, some per session. Some social services departments have developed training in basic financial calculations for care management staff who are dealing with budgets for the first time. Consider requesting this if you know it would help. See also Chapter 7.

Justifying the cost of the care plan to the budget-holder

Principal care manager: 'We have rapidly learnt from our early mistakes that if you pay peanuts you get monkeys. The best shouldn't mean the cheapest, it should mean the best quality within the available budget.'

The budget for the care package may need to be agreed with your budget-holder before it is finalised with the user, especially if it is above a specified level, or includes an expensive or non-standard option. The budget-holder may be under pressure to keep costs down, and may apply the same pressure to you. You must be prepared to present detailed information about added value to justify your decision. Remember to identify the risks and social costs to compare with financial costs. If the budget-holder still does not accept your costs, ask for your concerns to be recorded. Keep in mind that you are accountable for your professional judgements.

- Can you accurately work out the weekly costs of a package of care services to support someone in their own home?
- Are you able to present clear, accurate and detailed information about added value to justify your choice of provider?

Negotiating the final care specification and price with the provider

The care plan should provide a specification of the care package/network of care services that will be delivered to the user. The details of each service or component of the care package need to be accurately specified to each supplier. For care management staff, this may involve sensitively adapting details of the core contract and service specification (developed centrally by the social services department's contracts manager and service planners) to each service user (see Chapter 4).

These fine details are an important part of the contract, as they ensure that the provider knows exactly what they are expected to deliver to the user. While one client tires easily and has to sleep in the afternoons, another is happy to receive domiciliary care or go to a day centre at any time during the day. Should the time of day for the first user be specified, or left to the discretion of the providing agency? If this detail is not specified, who is responsible if the service user is unable to benefit from care arranged in the afternoon? See Chapter 5 for further discussion about what kind of detail care management staff should specify.

Providers have different systems for pricing their services. They may offer:

- a general or standardised price, based on the average price for supplying services to clients with different levels of need;
- price bands for clients with lower and higher levels of need;
- a core price, with added itemised charges for specific needs.

There is some debate about the advantages and disadvantages of these different pricing systems to purchasers and users. The important point to remember is that, whatever their pricing system, providers hope to sell their services. It is always worth checking whether a provider is open to some degree of negotiation over the quoted price and what it covers.

Although some traditional aspects of social work involve negotiating skills, many front-line workers do not like negotiating prices with providers. This is understandable, but ultimately not helpful to your clients. Learning to extend existing negotiating skills can help you to get a better deal for service users. It is also important because some providers may themselves use high-pressure negotiating techniques with front-line workers, clients and their families. You may not want to use such techniques yourself, but you need to recognise them and know how to deal with them. It is also important to deal fairly with less 'business-minded' providers, who through lack of experience may leave themselves open to exploitation. Negotiating skills are dealt with fully in Chapter 8.

CHECK YOUR OWN PRACTICE

■ How confident are you about negotiating details to get the right service at the right price?

Understanding the contract and explaining it to users

The contract is an agreement between the purchaser and the provider and as such it is a method of regulating the quality of service provided. It should be designed to protect users against unsatisfactory or unscrupulous providers. The core terms and conditions of contracts are normally drawn up by the social services contracts manager and legal staff, but it is important that workers who arrange individual services understand the purpose of the contract and can explain it to users. Contracts are explained fully in Chapter 4.

CHECK YOUR OWN PRACTICE

■ Do you understand the purpose of the contract?

■ Can you explain the contract to users in terms that they can understand?

MONITORING AND REVIEW

Monitoring means systematically checking how the care plan is working in practice. You need to know that the services you have arranged or purchased for the user are being delivered, that they are being delivered to satisfactory standards, and that they are achieving the intended outcomes. Monitoring should take place regularly: care management cannot be effective without it.

Monitoring should be separated from provision: the provider may be asked to monitor aspects of service delivery, but the person who oversees the monitoring should be independent of the provider. There are advantages if the person who does the needs assessment also monitors provision, but it is not essential.

Review is an essential aspect of monitoring. The care package, or network of services arranged to support the client, needs to be flexible; it may need to adapt or evolve to meet the user's needs as they change over time. There must be systems for reviewing the initial care plan and checking which objectives or outcomes have been achieved, whether the plan is still appropriate to the user's needs, and which objectives or outcomes should be modified in the light of changing needs.

Systems for review vary with the nature of the care plan. A review for a user who receives one or two minor services could be carried out by letter or phone, but for users who have specialised or complex needs, a meeting of the different professionals and services involved may be essential. Social services departments are required by law to review services to certain groups of service users. You should know how this legal duty is translated into review policy and practice in your authority.

Review arrangements should be set out at the time the care plan is agreed; further action, and the person responsible for action, should be recorded after each review.

CHECK YOUR OWN PRACTICE

- How do you monitor delivery of the care services you arrange or purchase?
- What methods do you use to review the care plan?

THE COSTS OF CARE MANAGEMENT

Assistant Director, Adult Services: 'About 15 per cent of our budget is spent on assessment, and requests for assessment are increasing. It is a balancing act – we don't want to end up with a lot of assessments and no services.'

Social services departments have to decide how to divide resources between care management and the provision of services. On the one hand, resources spent on care management cannot be spent on provision. On the other hand, good care management is cost-effective because it helps to shape the range, flexibility and quality of providers, and so increases choice and flexibility of services for users. It also helps to ensure that money is not spent on ineffective services.

Social services departments need to cost their care management arrangements accurately, and to keep these costs to a reasonable level. Care management is itself a service which must give value for money. This means balancing quality (of the service you provide to users) with productivity (the number of cases you are able to manage).

Managers tend to concentrate on productivity; front-line workers see this as reducing the quality of service. This is one reason why it is important for care management staff to understand and take an active part in the development of quality assurance systems (see Chapter 6). A poor quality assurance system can be a management euphemism for imposing productivity targets: a well-designed quality assurance system should provide the right mechanisms for consulting users and front-line workers, and negotiating a workable balance between productivity and quality.

This chapter has provided an extended checklist to help you review the topics that you would like to know more about and the skills that you would like to develop. The following chapters look in more detail at understanding contracts, using the care plan as a specification, quality assurance, financial skills and negotiating. The final chapter sets out an action plan which you can use to help you identify areas in which you would like further information or training. Now that you have worked through the questions in this chapter, you may find it useful to start making notes on the action plan.

RECOMMENDED READING

■ *Assessing Needs and Planning Care in Social Work* (1993) Brian Taylor and Toni Devine, Arena. A clear, practical guide to the social work skills (but not business skills) needed in assessment and care planning, and underpinning theory.

■ *Care Management and Assessment: Practitioners' Guide* (1991) Department of Health Social Services Inspectorate, Scottish Office Social Work Services Group, HMSO. Official guidance for practitioners.

■ *Devising and Resourcing Personal Care Packages* (1995) Flora Gathorne-Hardy, available from Disablement Income Group, Unit 5, Archway Business Centre, 19–23 Wedmore Street, London N19 4RZ. An excellent short, practical guide to planning and sourcing care for people with disabilities.

■ *Handbook for Assessing and Managing Care in the Community* (1994) Philip Seed and Gillian Kaye, Jessica Kingsley. Discusses different approaches to assessment and care management, drawing on recent research to develop care management methods suitable for adults with learning difficulties.

■ *Purchasing and Contracting Skills* (1995) David Best, CCETSW. A guide for social work education and training, this report covers ethical issues in purchasing and contracting, purchasing tasks and processes, and contracting relationships, and sets out competences to be covered within a training curriculum.

Other official guidance referred to in this chapter

■ *Care Management and Assessment: Managers' Guide* (1991) Department of Health Social Services Inspectorate, Scottish Office Social Work Services Group, HMSO.

■ *Community Care in the Next Decade and Beyond: Policy Guidance* (1990) HMSO.

4 Understanding contracts

The aim of this chapter is to enable you to understand and use community care contracts effectively. The first part of the chapter briefly summarises key principles of contract law that are relevant to care management. The second part looks at the different components of community care contracts and why they are important, and describes the different types of contract that care managers are likely to use. The final part explains the importance of contract specification for ensuring quality outcomes for service users, and discusses how you can make sure that contracts provide protection for your clients.

QUESTIONS THIS CHAPTER WILL TRY TO ANSWER

- What is a contract, and why are contracts necessary in community care?
- What are the typical components of a community care contract, and what is their purpose?
- What is meant by block, cost-and-volume and spot contracts? How are they used?
- How do contracts protect service users?
- What happens if the provider breaches a contract?

Contracts for social care are not new, but the Government's wish to promote a mixed economy of care makes it necessary for social services departments to enter into contracts with external providers on a much wider scale than previously, in order to purchase care services. Generally the social services contracts manager will negotiate the main terms of contracts and provide standard contract forms to be used for one-off purchases. Care management staff are responsible for entering important administrative details and for specifying individual care needs in that section of the contract which relates to the individual client. The more your authority favours devolved responsibility and contract flexibility, the greater will be your involvement in negotiating contracts.

Because contracts are legally enforceable agreements, it is important to understand what they are and how to use them. This chapter looks at the broad principles. Chapter 5 provides information on tailoring contracts to individual care needs. Negotiating contracts is covered in Chapter 8.

CONTRACT LAW

The law of contract is central to business activities because it provides the legal framework for business agreements. There is an extensive body of legal precedent and statute law, and its detailed interpretation is a matter for legal experts. It is, however, useful to be familiar with the general principles: this will help you to understand why the community care contracts you come across are framed in the way that they are and why it is important to get the detail right. Note that this section covers only English law of contract. Scottish law is different.

A contract is an agreement between two or more parties, which the parties intend to be legally binding and which can be legally enforced. In English law there must be **consideration**: each party must pay some sort of price for the obligations of the others (for example, one party agrees to provide services in exchange for payments by the other party).

A contract may not be legally binding where there is:

Misrepresentation – misrepresentation of the true facts by one or more parties to the contract.

Fundamental mistake – such as getting the identities of the parties wrong.

Lack of capacity – the incapacity of a party to the contract to understand the agreement, because of disability or intoxication by drugs or alcohol.

Illegality – where what is agreed to is illegal.

Coercion – where one party forces the other to agree.

What is agreed should be specified in the terms of the contract. These terms generally consist of written or spoken statements agreed to by the parties to the contract. Note that, except in certain special cases, a contract does not have to be written. It is quite possible to have a verbal contract, and in some cases a contract can be implied by the conduct of the parties – when you buy goods in a shop, for example, a contract is established between you and the trader. Business contracts are generally written so that the terms of the contract can be identified: if you cannot identify the terms of a contract, you cannot identify whether a breach has occurred and so will be unable to enforce it.

If a breach of contract occurs, the aggrieved party can seek a remedy through the law. If the case is proved, the remedy may take two forms: the court may order that money should be paid in compensation, known as **damages**, or, if it is fair and reasonable to do so, the court may instruct the defaulting party to fulfil the obligations of the contract by means of an **injunction** or a **decree of specific performance**.

To summarise, a contract is a legally enforceable agreement between clearly identified parties to carry out the terms of the contract for a consideration. Failure by one party to fulfil the terms constitutes a breach for which the aggrieved party can seek a legally enforceable remedy.

CONTRACTS FOR CARE SERVICES

Where social services departments identify particular needs in the community, service planners often develop a **service specification** for those needs. This sets out the minimum service requirements that the department considers adequate to meet the needs identified (see pp 87–88).

Negotiations with service providers are based on the department's service specifications. Individual contractors may opt to deliver only some of the services covered in the service specification. For example, a provider may agree to provide home care services as set out in the specification by day, but not by night. Once the contractor agrees to provide this service, they must comply with the requirements in the service specification, which is attached to the contract.

Through a combination of directly provided services and contracts, the social services department will seek to ensure that all the services in the department's service specification are provided. An authority may buy in services from several contractors (for example, one to provide home care by day, another for care by night) in order to make up a care package for an individual.

In addition to the service specification, contracts for community care services will include the **contract conditions** (the terms agreed between the parties for the operation of the contract itself; see pp 75–76) and the **individual service contract** (which sets out the service to be provided to the individual user; see p 76).

Standardising contracts and reducing transaction costs

Drawing up contracts costs time and resources for everyone involved: these are known as **transaction costs**. The Association of Metropolitan Authorities (AMA), Association of County Councils (ACC) and Association of Directors of Social Services (ADSS) therefore favour standardising the contracting process, in collaboration with users (see p 77). This would help to ensure that contracts provide adequate protection for service users, and minimise the transaction costs. (Every pound spent on transaction costs means one pound less available for service provision.) AMA, ACC and ADSS guidance recommends model contracts which have these standard features:

- pre-purchase agreement
- service specification
- individual service contract

The pre-purchase agreement

This is an agreement between the local authority and the service provider establishing an option to purchase services. It contains the contract conditions (see below) and clearly states that the purpose of the contract is to deliver the service specification.

The contract conditions

These identify the terms agreed between the parties for the operation of the contract itself. They generally cover:

- the duration of the contract;

- purchasing arrangements;
- identification of the services which the contract covers (usually a clause stating that the conditions in the attached service specification are part of the contract);
- an agreed variation procedure;
- arrangements for dealing with unpredicted costs and inflation;
- a procedure for resolving any problems or disputes;
- default arrangements;
- insurance cover;
- the authorised officers;
- details of subcontracting;
- details of complaints procedures;
- means of monitoring;
- an agreed review procedure.

The service specification

This identifies the features of the service to be provided (see Chapter 5). It is an essential part of the contract and is attached to it as a schedule (an appended document). According to Government guidance, the service or contract specification 'identifies what services are to be provided and is based on the social services department service specification' (*Purchase of Service*, para 4.3.8). Appendix 2 is an example of a specification for domiciliary care services.

The individual service contract (ISC)

The ISC is the document that links the pre-purchase agreement to an individual care plan. This is the part of the contract which is dealt with by care management staff. It activates the provision of a service for an identified individual. It, too, should be a schedule to the pre-purchase agreement and should give 'precise details of the services to be provided with details of the time and agreed cost. The ISC should reflect the contents of the care plan. If services are to be provided by different Service Providers, it will be necessary to issue more than one ISC' (*Guidance on Contracting for Domiciliary and Day Care Services*, p 102).

HOW STANDARDISED CONTRACTS ARE DEVELOPED AND ACTIVATED

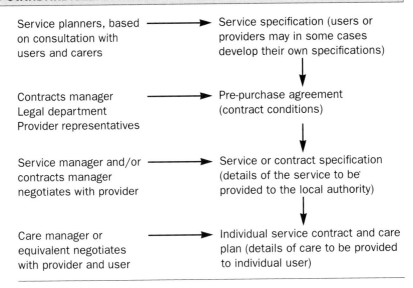

Service planners, based on consultation with users and carers ⟶ Service specification (users or providers may in some cases develop their own specifications)

Contracts manager Legal department Provider representatives ⟶ Pre-purchase agreement (contract conditions)

Service manager and/or contracts manager negotiates with provider ⟶ Service or contract specification (details of the service to be provided to the local authority)

Care manager or equivalent negotiates with provider and user ⟶ Individual service contract and care plan (details of care to be provided to individual user)

CHECK THE LOCAL AUTHORITY PRACTICE

- How does the standardised three-part contract described here compare with contracts used in your authority?
- Are the arrangements for developing contracts and contracting for individual services in your authority similar to the general principles set out here or are they significantly different?

TYPES OF CONTRACT

Local authorities generally use three types of contract for the purchase of care:

- block contracts
- cost-and-volume contracts
- spot contracts

Block contracts

Block contracts are agreements that a stated volume of specified services will be provided for a fixed price. They provide certainty for both service purchaser and service provider: the purchaser knows how much the service is going to cost, the provider knows what income to expect. Block contracts may, however, lack flexibility and could reduce the quality of care for the service user – tending towards provision that is service-led rather than needs-led. A block contract may also commit the purchaser to paying for more services than are actually used. Large block contracts may bring efficiencies of scale but could also reduce diversity of provision by stifling competition. Small block contracts, on the other hand, can stimulate new entrants to the market by guaranteeing their income, and thereby increasing the choice of services available to the user.

Cost-and-volume contracts

Cost-and-volume contracts allow greater flexibility than block contracts by guaranteeing that a specified minimum volume of services will be provided at a fixed cost and giving the purchaser the option to buy extra units at an agreed price. This combines a measure of security and flexibility for both purchaser and provider. Of course, the success of this type of contract depends on the social services department correctly identifying the level at which to set the guaranteed minimum.

Spot contracts

Spot contracts, also called price-per-case contracts, make agreements to purchase services on a case-by-case basis. They are often used by local authorities for purchasing residential or nursing home care. They may be negotiated from scratch on each occasion or negotiated on the basis of standardised contracts. Spot contracts would appear to offer the greatest flexibility and encourage the greatest competition. But because they give providers little security they can distort the structure of the local care market, discouraging new entrants and encouraging existing providers to limit their capacity.

Informal agreements

Besides formal, legally binding contracts with service providers, some local authorities encourage care management staff to initiate informal agreements with carers or neighbours as part of the care plan for service users. These agreements are best dealt with by a simple exchange of letters confirming the service to be provided and the amount to be paid. Putting the agreement in writing helps everyone involved to be clear about what has been agreed. It also provides you with a record of the agreement if facts need to be checked at some later date. Some authorities are opposed to such arrangements. Check that you are fully aware of your own authority's policy on informal arrangements.

An arrangement at this level would not generally be regarded as legally binding by the parties to it, and so would not constitute a contract. To ensure that informal agreements are made in a consistent way by front-line workers, and that vulnerable users are protected, your authority should provide clear guidelines on when and how this type of arrangement can be used.

Despite moves towards standardisation, the form of contracts, the conditions they contain and the procedures for using them vary widely from one authority to another. It is important to understand the principles behind your social services department's contracting arrangements, as well as the bureaucratic procedures and details of form-filling. If you would like more information or explanation about how the principles set out here are applied in practice in your authority, the contracts manager will be a good source of information.

CHECK THE LOCAL AUTHORITY PRACTICE

- Which of the three types of contract described above are used by your social services department?

- If different types of contract are used for different services, do you know why?

- Does your authority promote the use of informal agreements? Are you familiar with guidance on the scope and limits of such agreements?

USING CONTRACTS

As a front-line worker involved in care management, you will be involved with handling that part of the contract which deals with services to the individual: the individual service contract if you are 'calling off' a block contract, or the equivalent part of a spot contract if your authority uses a standardised spot contract form. This section briefly discusses some legal and technical aspects of using contracts that you should be aware of. It is important that you:

- understand how your authority checks the quality of providers with whom you contract;

- enter important details accurately on the contract;

- are aware of the implications of two-way and three-way contracts;

- act promptly if you suspect a breach of contract.

Understand how your authority checks the quality of providers

Your choice of providers will be limited by legal requirements and to a greater or lesser extent by the local authority's checks on quality.

Residential homes

These must by law be registered with a social services department and homes for four or more people must be inspected annually. The social services registration and inspection unit staff can tell you in detail about registration standards that homes must meet. (Nursing homes must be registered and inspected by the health authority.)

Non-residential care services

There is at present no legal requirement to inspect or register domiciliary or day care services. To check the quality of potential providers, some social services departments operate **accreditation systems**. These are quality asssurance systems which ensure that the service provider is aware of the standards of service that the local authority requires, and has systems in place to see that those standards are met. If your authority operates an accreditation system, you may be instructed to select only accredited providers.

Some authorities simply operate **listings** or confusingly named '**registration**' schemes for non-residential providers. These are often little more than lists of possible providers. They provide no guarantee of quality, and should be regarded as voluntary – they are simply a convenience to help front-line workers to identify possible providers. Do not confuse 'registration' schemes for non-residential providers with the registration and inspection of residential homes.

If your authority does not have an accreditation system for non-residential services, you need to exercise extra care when agreeing contracts with these providers.

Enter important details accurately

On the individual service contract (ISC), or its equivalent, it is important to get right key details such as the identities of the service user, purchaser and provider and the duration of the contract. If they are not correct the contract may be void.

The ISC is the main means of tailoring the general contract agreed with the provider to the individual needs of the service user, so care is needed in specifying the services to be provided to ensure that the service user's needs are being met. It is good practice to append a copy of the care plan to the ISC so that everyone is aware of its contents.

Be clear about the implications of two-way and three-way contracts

If the service user is a party to the contract, his or her signature should be on the contract along with the service purchaser's and the service provider's. This gives the service user the right to sue the other parties for breach of contract over any terms of the contract. If the user is not party to the contract, only the service purchaser can pursue a breach of contract by the service provider.

If the service user is to be a party to the contract, the user must agree to some form of 'consideration' (ie obligation to the other parties – see p 73). Consideration can be established by:

■ payment by the user to either the provider or the purchaser (which may be waived after means-testing);

■ agreement by the user to take on obligations under the terms of the contract (for example agreeing to allow a provider access to their home);

■ acceptance by the user that the service provider will meet their care needs.

The contract should contain specific references to the obligations that the service user accepts in exchange for the other two parties being bound by the terms of the contract. AMA/ACC/ADSS guidance suggests the following form of words:

> In exchange for the Service User agreeing to accept provision of the Service by the Service Provider, and making the specified payment (if any), the Service Purchaser and Service Provider each guarantee the Service User that they will carry our their respective obligations as set out in the main Contract as varied from time to time.
>
> *Guidance on Contracting for Domiciliary and Day Care Services*, p 46

Act promptly if you suspect a breach of contract

What are your responsibilities if you come across persistent shortcomings in a provider? In well-designed contracts, the service specification requires service providers to set up their own internal systems for quality assurance and quality control. Care management staff also have a responsibility to monitor the delivery of the service to the individual user, as part of their care management role. You should ensure that there are adequate monitoring, evaluation and review procedures to identify failings in the delivery of services at an early stage. As well as these formal procedures, informal feedback from service users and colleagues, and your own eyes and ears, will help you to assess the quality of service.

Where there are failings, your first course of action should be to try and find solutions in cooperation with the provider and service user. If this does not produce satisfactory results, you should seek advice from your line manager or contracts manager. Remember that the duty to provide care rests with the local authority and this duty is not discharged by signing a contract with a service provider. If a provider fails to meet important conditions, this may be a breach of contract which could lead to legal action. If you believe that a provider may be failing to meet essential conditions (as opposed to minor ones – see below), raise your concerns with the provider; keep an accurate record of difficulties and action taken right from the start, and notify your line manager straight away.

SERVICE QUALITY AND MONITORING

The contract is a primary means of ensuring the quality of service to service users. It will be most successful if service users are engaged in the process of contract development at every stage:

- defining needs and priorities;
- setting overall service specifications;
- tailoring services to individual needs;
- identifying key standards and outcomes;
- designing monitoring and review systems.

For care management staff it is crucial to ensure that the care plan provides enough detail to tailor the contract to individual needs. The key to successful outcomes is close consultation with the service user to develop the details of the care plan, to translate these as necessary into a specification for individual care in the ISC, and to select the appropriate service provider.

The need for care in choosing service providers cannot be overemphasised. Before you select, it is good practice to check that the provider is able to offer the required range of services. This is perhaps the most powerful means that most care management staff have of ensuring that services match needs. Having taken care to check that services are available, it is equally important to make sure that the services to be delivered are precisely stated in the individual service contract.

Monitoring and reviewing services is the only way of ensuring that the services actually provided are appropriate and match the provision specified in the contract. In services where there is no inspection (such as domiciliary and day care services), it is essential that review procedures are meaningful and do not degenerate into paper exercises. These are worse than useless because they give relatives, carers, administrators and politicians a false sense of security, allowing abuse of vulnerable users to go unchecked. Monitoring and review procedures are generally developed at management level, but there should be opportunities for front-line workers to contribute their views on making the procedures work well in practice.

CHECK THE LOCAL AUTHORITY PRACTICE

- Does your social services department provide guidance on your role in monitoring the contract, and what to do if you or the service user encounters difficulties with a provider?

- Do you use three-way (tripartite) contracts to which service users are a party? What forms of consideration by service users appear in these contracts?

- Does your authority operate an accreditation or registration system for providers of non-residential services? Do you fully understand the system and what criteria (if any) providers must meet in order to be listed?

- What methods do you use to check regularly that the services provided to the individual user match those which have been contracted for?

Care management staff need appropriate systems and guidance to help them select good-quality providers, handle contracts for individual care effectively, and ensure that they are working. At the time of writing, these systems are better developed in some authorities than others. You may find it helpful to talk to your line manager, the contracts officer or the person who deals with registration or accreditation, if you would like more detailed information or guidance on these issues.

This chapter has looked at key general principles that you need to be aware of if you use contracts in care management. Now that you have worked through the chapter, you may have identified areas in which you feel that further information or training would be useful. You may want to note these in the action plan section of Chapter 10. The next chapter discusses some useful principles to help you tailor the contract to meet individual care needs.

OFFICIAL GUIDANCE REFERRED TO IN THIS CHAPTER

- *Guidance on Contracting for Domiciliary and Day Care Services* (1995) Association of Metropolitan Authorities, Association of County Councils, Association of Directors of Social Services, published by Local Government Management Board.

- *Purchase of Service: Practice Guidance and practice material for social services departments and other agencies* (1991) Department of Health Social Services Inspectorate, HMSO.

5 Tailoring the contract to individual needs

The aim of this chapter is to explain the purpose of a specification, and to discuss what level of detail is needed to write a good care plan, which is in effect a specification for individual care. The first part of this chapter looks at the **service specification**, that section of the contract which sets out details of the service that the provider will supply to the local authority. The second part looks at the **individual service contract**, which sets out details of the care that will be provided to the individual user.

(The terms used in this chapter are those suggested in guidance prepared by the local authorities associations (see pp 75–77). The principles discussed here apply to any contract for social care, but you may need to check whether your own local authority uses different terms to describe the different parts of a contract and their contents.)

QUESTIONS THIS CHAPTER WILL TRY TO ANSWER

- What is a service specification and why is it important?
- What is the relationship between the service specification, the individual service contract and the care plan?
- What are the features of a well-written specification?
- What level of detail should be specified in the individual service contract and care plan?

WHAT IS A SERVICE SPECIFICATION AND WHY IS IT IMPORTANT?

Contracts officer: 'If you wanted to buy a car, you would make a list of the sort of things you were looking for: size of engine, petrol consumption, safety features, colour perhaps. You might decide that some features were essential, and some weren't. That's your own specification and you look for a car that matches it as closely as possible. Then you negotiate a price and the fine details with the dealer. He may give you some discount because he wants your business, but you may also want certain features that you're prepared to pay extra for. It's a similar process – the service specification gives you a yardstick for measuring providers and for providers to measure themselves against; it is the basis for negotiating the fine details and price that go in the contract. But the difference here is that the local authority is the "customer", not the service user. That makes it all more complicated.'

The **service specification** is a set of minimum requirements for a service that is to be supplied. Government guidance says that it is good practice for social services departments to develop general service specifications for all services, whether these are directly provided or purchased from external providers (*Purchase of Service*, 1991, para 3.2.2).

The local authority's service specification provides the basis for the social services department to negotiate contracts with providers. A provider may agree to adopt the specification as it stands or may be able to deliver only parts of it. In this case, the general service specification can be adapted to form the **contract specification** (also referred to as a service specification), which sets out precise details of the service that the provider agrees to supply to the local authority.

You need to be familiar with the contents of service specifications if you are involved in care planning. The care plan is the tool which enables care management staff to tailor the service specification to meet individual needs; it is a key part of the contracting process (*Guidance on Contracting for Domiciliary and Day Care Services*, p 101). You cannot use the care plan to tailor the service to individual needs unless you know what general terms are set out in the service specification.

In some authorities, service specifications are developed centrally and not normally circulated to front-line workers. Discuss with your line manager whether it would be good practice to have reference copies of relevant specifications for your team or locality office.

User and carer involvement

Users, carers and other relevant people should be involved in drawing up service specifications, through representative bodies such as users' or carers' groups. If users and carers want different things from a service, the specification should try to achieve an acceptable balance between their interests. To ensure that the service is equally accessible and appropriate to all sections of the community, the full range of potential users should be consulted. Black and ethnic minority users and carers must be properly represented.

Providers' involvement

If users have specialised needs calling for a provider with specialist experience or knowledge (for example day care for partially sighted older Asian people), it may be appropriate for the providing organisation to draft its own service specification. This can then be developed in collaboration with the local authority to provide the basis of the contract with the social services department.

CHECK THE LOCAL AUTHORITY'S PRACTICE

■ Are you familiar with the service specifications for residential, domiciliary and day care services that the social services department purchases?

■ What influence have users and carers had in shaping local service specifications?

■ Have any specifications been developed by providers themselves?

Talk to your line manager, contracts department or service planning officers for more information.

WHAT GOES INTO THE SERVICE SPECIFICATION?

This section explains key elements of the service specification in more detail. Appendix 2 is a sample specification for home care services; you may find it useful to read the information in this section alongside that, or alongside an actual service specification from your own social services department.

Government guidance issued in 1991 suggested that there are eight key elements that should be considered in any service specification, although the importance of each element varies with the nature of the service. These elements are:

- the context, or background, to the specification (eg why the service is needed);

- objectives of the service;

- inputs (resources allocated to the service – money, staff, equipment);

- process (the caring tasks or activities to be carried out);

- outputs (quantity of service to be provided – eg six hours' day care three times per week for 40 service users);

- outcomes (the results – how the service will contribute to the well-being of the user);

- quality (the standards of service required);

- monitoring (service standards and results).

Specifying inputs, process, outputs and outcomes

Describing social care services in terms of inputs, process, outputs and outcomes is an approach which has been adapted from business management and the commercial production of goods and services. Purchasers, providers and front-line workers need a shared understanding of these terms, because you will need to decide whether the input, process, output or outcome is most important to the individual care plan and what sort of detail to specify.

TERMS USED IN SERVICE SPECIFICATIONS AND WHAT THEY MEAN	EXAMPLES FROM SPECIFICATIONS FOR VARIOUS KINDS OF SERVICE
Objectives Aims and general purpose of the service	**An ethnic minority users' group** *To provide information and support for potential elderly service users and their carers in the Bangladeshi community, and to increase their access to a range of community care services*
Quality The specification should state the required standards for inputs, outputs and outcomes, and how these are to be measured	**A day centre** *The service provider must have in place a formal system of quality assurance with a written policy setting out expectations, standards and systems of verification and feedback. The local authority will require access to the system for monitoring purposes*
It should refer to existing standards, guidelines or codes of practice	**A home care service** *The service provider must meet the standards contained in the United Kingdom Home Care Association's Code of Practice*
Input Resources to be allocated for an activity or process, eg money, staff, equipment	**A day centre** *Service providers must ensure that they have sufficient staff, both in numbers and with appropriate skills or qualifications, to meet the needs of service users* **A home care service** *Equipment belonging to the user but used by the service provider (such as lifts, hoists, electrical equipment) must be maintained in a safe condition*
Process/activity What the provider does with the resources: – the care/helping process – activities/ tasks to be carried out	**A home care service** *The services to be provided will include washing, bathing, hair care, denture and mouth care, foot care (but not care which requires a State-registered chiropodist)*

Output
The results of the activity/quantity of service to be provided, numbers to be catered for, how often. Measurable units of service delivered to clients

A disability advice service
The service provider will provide 30 hours of face-to-face and telephone advice (2 workers × 15 hours each) between 9.30 am and 12.30 pm, Mondays to Fridays, at the Nelson Mandela Centre

Outcome
Results or effects of the process or output, ie the contribution to the well-being of the client

A home care service
The desired outcome of the service is to provide adequate support when the person wishes to stay in their own home in order to prevent admission to residential or nursing home care

The advantage of specifying services in these terms is that it enables service planners to analyse more closely the way in which particular services achieve results. Similar outcomes or results can be achieved by different levels of input (a voluntary organisation may offer the same quality of domiciliary personal care at lower cost than a commercial agency) or different kinds of activity (respite care to give the carer a break could be provided in the user's home, hospital, a nursing home or a foster carer's home). Services with apparently similar inputs, carrying out similar activities, may achieve very different results (one advocacy scheme may deal with fewer clients but have greater success in achieving clients' objectives than another centre with similar levels of funding and staff).

Comparing inputs, process, outputs and outcomes enables service planners to evaluate more accurately what factors contribute to satisfactory results, and which services are efficient at achieving these. It can help to identify those providers that offer the best combination of quality and cost-effective services. It can help to identify the reasons for unsatisfactory outcomes, and providers or aspects of services that do not represent good value.

The disadvantage of this approach is that when social services budgets are shrinking, budget-holding managers may be forced to concentrate on what volume of output can be achieved for the available input (what is the maximum amount of day or domiciliary care we can purchase with our already overstretched budget?) rather than on the quality of the process and outcomes for individual users. Care management staff need to ensure that the individual service contract and attached care plan specify the inputs, process and outcomes for the individual user in a way that ensures quality of care and visible results for the user in terms of improving or maintaining quality of life.

Developing standardised specifications

In practice, specifications for different kinds of care service vary enormously. They inevitably vary because of local circumstances and the nature of the service, but at present even specifications for similar services tend to vary between local authorities in the range and amount of detail covered, and in the way this is set out. This can be time-consuming for service planners and contracts managers. It is also confusing for providers, who may be negotiating contracts for similar services with different authorities.

In 1995 the Association of Metropolitan Authorities, Association of County Councils and Association of Directors of Social Services sought to draw together existing experience and help reduce confusion for providers by publishing a jointly agreed document, *Guidance on Contracting for Domiciliary and Day Care Services*. This develops some of the principles in the 1991 Government guidance and sets out a more comprehensive framework for the range of information and level of detail that should be included in service specifications. Most local authorities have broadly adopted the suggested framework for specifications in the AMA/ACC/ADSS guidance. Here is one contracts officer's adapted version of the suggested framework for domiciliary care specifications:

Background Why is the service needed? Who is it for? Who has been consulted? How does it fit in with legislation/local policy, etc?

Principles What are the principles or values on which the service is based?

Aims or objectives What is the service seeking to achieve?

Details of the service required What tasks or activities is the service to consist of?

Priority/eligibility for the service Who is the service for? (The description should include the local authority's own eligibility criteria.)

Recruitment and training What arrangements must the provider have in place to select, train and employ staff?

General conduct Policy on misconduct, receiving gifts, handling users' money, etc.

Confidentiality Policy on safeguarding personal information disclosed to the provider.

Users at risk What does 'at risk' mean? What are the provider's legal duties towards a user at risk? What procedures should be followed?

Quality standards What standards must the provider meet?

Outcomes How will the service benefit users?

Monitoring How will the quality of tasks, activities and outcomes be checked?

Health and safety What are the provider's legal responsibilities for the health and safety of their staff and service users?

Information for service users What specific information will be provided, to what standards?

Features of a well-written specification

So far we have discussed what goes into the specification, but how it is written is also important. It should be clear, accessible and understandable so that:

- It enables the provider to design services that meet the requirements.
- It tells users clearly what they can expect from the service.

A specification will work well only if users are satisfied that what is specified is appropriate to their needs, and if the provider has enough detail to know what is expected. If the specification is too prescriptive, the provider may be discouraged from taking initiative on issues which fall outside the inputs or activities that are specified. So it should cover essential requirements, but flexibly. If it is too vague, the purchaser has no way of measuring whether the provider is delivering a satisfactory service. The example below shows how a general aim is developed into a detailed specification of the activities that the service provider must carry out.

BALANCING CLARITY, FLEXIBILITY AND NECESSARY DETAIL

Specification	Comment
The service will provide personal care to help service users maintain independence in their own home	*Too vague. Needs more detail*
↓	
Personal care will include tasks which could be undertaken by family carers	*Gives a clearer idea of the nature and range of services, without being prescriptive, but is wide open to different interpretations*
↓	
It excludes nursing care, which is the responsibility of the health service	*If services are paid for from different budgets, it is important to specify what is not required*
↓	
The services to be provided will include but are not confined to:	*Helpful to specify the nature of essential tasks, while leaving room for flexibility*
■ Assisting the service user to get up or go to bed. This service should be undertaken within half an hour of a time specified by the user	*Some services are not time-specific, but it is essential to specify services which are, and to specify the limits of acceptable flexibility*
■ Assisting the user with taking medication which has been prescribed. This should be done in accordance with health authority and local authority policy and procedure. Please see attached guidelines	*If the activity must be carried out according to legal requirements, local policy or guidelines, this must be clearly specified*

Source Adapted from *Guidance on Contracting for Domiciliary and Day Care Services*, pp 53–54.

Social welfare officer: 'The care plan said that the putting to bed service should be at a time agreed between the agency and the user, who asked for 10 o'clock. At the six-week review we discovered that the agency's carer was arriving up to an hour and a quarter each side, so one night my client went to bed at 8.45 and the next at 11.15. I'd never been given a copy of the contract specification, but at that point my line manager told me that it stated "the service to be provided within half an hour of the time specified by the user". If the user and I had seen the specification, it could have been sorted out at the start, rather than going on for weeks.'

CHECK THE LOCAL AUTHORITY'S PRACTICE

- Read over one or two examples of local service specifications for the services you arrange for clients. How clear and accessible are they to users and providers?
- Do they clearly specify inputs, process or activities, outputs and outcomes?
- Do they clearly set out quality standards?
- Are there any parts of the specification that you don't understand?
- Are there any terms and conditions that could affect the way in which you specify the individual care required in the care plan?

WHAT GOES INTO THE INDIVIDUAL SERVICE CONTRACT?

The pre-purchase agreement and service or contract specification cover the general terms and conditions that providers agree to when they accept a contract for any service user (see Chapter 4). These documents provide a general framework which is legally binding and designed to protect all service users, but they cannot deal with the specific needs of individual service users.

Specification for individual care

The **individual service contract (ISC)** is the document which allows care management staff to tailor the contract to the needs of the individual identified in the assessment. It is based on the care plan drawn up by the front-line worker. The ISC and care plan together provide a specification for individual care. The ISC should describe the specific services to be provided to the individual, and state the desired outcomes of these services. It should list precise details, including time and agreed cost. Where appropriate, a copy of the care plan should be attached to the ISC and form part of it (*Guidance on Contracting for Domiciliary and Day Care Services*, pp 30, 46).

It is not possible to say precisely what details will be most important in any individual service contract. This will vary with the nature of the service and the needs of the individual. The points below seek to draw together sound professional practice in care planning and good practice in business specification. Not all will be relevant to each individual service contract, but you may find them useful to refer to.

User involvement

You should aim to involve the service user or their representative as fully as possible in the process of agreeing the individual service contract. If the ISC is a three-way agreement between local authority, service provider and service user, you must explain the contents fully before asking the user to sign it. This can help to ensure that the contract ties up with the care plan. If the ISC is a two-way agreement, it is essential to involve the service user in completing the care plan and to check that the user is satisfied that the details in the ISC accurately reflect the care plan.

Technical details

Parties to the contract

A contract document must specify who the contract is between, ie the local authority and the provider. This may seem a small detail, but if you forget to enter the provider's name on the individual service contract, or get it wrong, it could mean that the contract is not legally valid.

A reference to general contract conditions

The individual service contract should contain a statement which makes it clear that the general terms and conditions set out in the pre-purchase agreement and service specification are part of the ISC, for example:

> This individual service contract is for the purchase of day care services in accordance with the conditions of the pre-purchase agreement with the service provider. The terms of the service specification are deemed to be incorporated in this ISC.

Your social services department may use a standard ISC form with wording along these lines. If not, you should check with your line manager or contracts department whether you need to enter this kind of statement yourself.

Minor changes in the contract

The ISC needs to be flexible enough to allow certain details (for example the time of delivery of a particular service) to be agreed between the provider and the service user without having to involve the purchaser. The ISC may also include a section which enables the purchaser and provider to make minor changes to the ISC by agreement (provided that this is recorded on the ISC and notified to the user), without first having to obtain the approval of the service user. Without such arrangements, minor changes can render the contract invalid.

SPECIFYING INDIVIDUAL CARE NEEDS

You may need to specify the details below either in the individual service contract or in the care plan. This varies according to the nature of the service, the type of contract, and the layout of ISC and care plan forms used by your local authority.

Terms used in care planning

Terms used in care planning vary from area to area, between different parts of the same service, and between the different professionals involved. 'Aim', 'objective', 'goal' and 'outcome' are used interchangeably by some people, but with very different and specific meanings by others. This section suggests some working definitions which may help you to focus on the central task, which is to specify clearly how the services you buy should benefit the user.

Aim: The general direction or purpose of the worker's and client's actions.

> **Example:** To reduce isolation.

An aim is often a long-term goal, which may seem to the user complicated or difficult to achieve. It is helpful to the user as well as to the care management worker and provider to try and break it down into objectives that are realistic and achievable. It may help to break a long-term goal into short-term stages, with objectives for each stage.

Objective: An achievable goal, described in terms of the proposed change for the person who is receiving a service.

Example: To enable Mr Saddiqui to have regular social contact with people who speak his own language and share his cultural background. (Mr Saddiqui lives alone and is disabled.)

This is more concrete, but does not describe what is to be achieved in terms that can be easily measured.

Outcome: The desired effect on the user's well-being, expressed as an observable or measurable change, either in behaviour or in the quality of care or in the user's quality of life. (Sometimes an objective is expressed in terms of a measurable change, so the objective and outcome are the same. Sometimes an objective needs further refining.)

Example: The user should have contact at least twice a week with other people who can communicate with him fully in his own first language.

He should be able to attend the mosque once a week.

He should be able to use a pay phone to talk to relatives in other parts of the country.

Specifying outcomes

You should try to define as clearly as possible the outcomes sought for the individual client. This allows you to measure the effectiveness of the service. It helps you to focus on what the user and carer want to achieve, and to think flexibly about different ways of getting there, rather than simply compiling a shopping list of required tasks.

WHO DECIDES THE OUTCOMES?

Specifying outcomes helps to improve the quality of care planning and arranging services, but bear in mind that people want different outcomes. Outcomes must be related to the needs assessment, so the debate about what is defined as a need and who defines it is relevant here.

The user may not want the same outcome as the carer. The carer might, for example, want the user to receive respite care away from home to give the whole family a break, while the user wants to be cared for at home because the idea of care from strangers in a strange place is deeply distressing. The front-line worker may know that the outcome sought by the user and carer is simply not feasible within the available budget. Or the front-line worker may make a professional judgement that the outcome sought by the user is not in his or her best interests (for example, where a user wishes to continue living at home but there is a serious risk to their own or others' safety).

It can be difficult to specify outcomes in terms that enable you to measure accurately the effect of services. Sometimes it is not easy to say how much a particular input or activity has contributed to the desired result and how much is due to other factors. For example, day care may improve the quality of life of a person with Alzheimer's disease not so much because of the day centre activities but because the break from caring reduces stress for the person's wife, and the support she receives from day centre staff greatly increases her confidence and ability to cope with caring for her husband.

Specifying inputs and activities

Once you and the service user are clear about the objectives and outcomes of the care plan, you can consider what action is needed to achieve each outcome you have listed. Various terms are used to describe the who, what, when and where of the action required. Money, staff and equipment or facilities may be described as 'resources' rather than 'inputs'. The specific care or support required may be described in terms of 'tasks', 'activities' or 'methods' rather than 'process'.

Considering options

If you start by specifying outcomes, it is easier to think flexibly about different ways of achieving them. To return to the example of Mr Saddiqui, regular contact with someone who speaks his own language might be achieved through day care at a local centre for Asian elders, through a Sylheti-speaking interpreter at a day centre catering for clients from a range of cultural backgrounds (who might also be the best person to teach him how to use a pay phone), through a formal arrangement with a Bangladeshi neighbour willing to visit for a couple of hours twice a week, or in summer through transport to take Mr Saddiqui to and from the local park, where his elderly Bangladeshi friends normally gather in the early afternoon to sit on the benches and talk.

Depending on the nature of the service, it may be helpful to define inputs and activities separately. For example, 'day care three times a week at Rosewell Centre' describes the input, but the specific activities to be carried out by day centre staff with an individual client will also need to be defined. In some cases, the distinction between input and activity may be blurred. If, for example, the objective is to help a severely disabled service user to have a bath, it will be necessary to specify how the user wil' be helped into and out of the bath. Here the input and activity are described together: 'Two care workers, trained in correct lifting procedure, to assist the client into and out of the bath, using the mechanical hoist provided.'

Flexible inputs or activities

The assessment may identify a need to work towards a particular outcome, but the inputs needed to achieve this will change over time. It may be preferable to specify that a client should achieve a certain outcome within a given period, but to allow the provider to vary or develop the methods or activities with the user's progress.

> **Example:** 'Day centre staff should establish a programme of activities designed to increase the mobility of the service user. It is expected that after three months the service user will be able to walk at least 10 yards unassisted.'

Closely defined inputs or activities

Some inputs or activities need to take place on a regular basis, or care workers may need explicit information if they are to carry out a task properly. Defining the input or activity in the right level of detail ensures that service providers know exactly what is expected; it also protects service users who are vulnerable, isolated or dependent, or who have difficulty communicating their needs and wishes.

> **Example:** A frail older person is able to remain fully continent only if she is encouraged to go to the toilet at specific intervals. 'The service user needs assistance with going to the toilet at regular intervals: the care worker must ensure that this interval is not more than two hours.'

> **Example:** A Jewish service user who is becoming increasingly confused needs help with shopping and preparing meals. 'The user needs help with getting shopping and preparing lunch. The service user is Jewish and the care worker should follow relatives' instructions about observing kashruth (keeping a kosher kitchen and buying and preparing kosher food).'

Putting it all together

The example below shows how the details of action agreed with a service user might be specified to the service provider. (There are of course other options for tackling the difficulties faced by the Thompsons – this is not presented as a model care plan, or the only course of action, but simply as an illustration.)

SAMPLE SPECIFICATION FOR INDIVIDUAL CARE

Joe Thompson, aged 68, had a stroke three months ago which left his left side partially paralysed and affected his speech. At present Joe refuses to leave the house, and is very withdrawn. His daughter Martha, who gave up work to care for him, rapidly became very depressed and contacted social services because she felt she could not cope much longer. The care manager introduced Martha to a carers' group, and is arranging for a home care agency to provide care two mornings a week so that Joe can get regular independent support with his rehabilitation programme and Martha can take a part-time job.

Aims
- To avoid admission to residential care.
- To help user to recover mobility and independence.
- To reduce level of stress experienced by carer.

Objectives
- To enable the user to carry out daily living activities on waking.
- To help user regain mobility in right leg and arm.
- To enable the carer to get a break from caring and maintain a part-time job.

Input
Care assistant 2 × 3 hours per week @ £5 per hour plus travel expenses, 8.30–11.30 am Tuesday and Thursday.
Must arrive by 8.30 am as daughter leaves for work at 8.35.

Activities
- Support user in getting out of bed, grooming, bathing, going to the toilet, getting dressed, preparing breakfast, washing up. Encourage user to use affected limbs and regain independence in these tasks.
- Assist with rehabilitation programme provided by physiotherapist. Carry out morning exercises as specified in physio programme.
- In collaboration with user and carer, keep a weekly record of progress with mobility.

Desired outcomes

- User enabled to carry out routine daily living activities independently of regular carer.

- User able to hold pencil and use cutlery in right hand and walk across the room without help after three months.

- Carers feels less unsupported, emotionally stronger and less stressed, enabled to continue caring.

CHECK YOUR OWN PRACTICE

- How do the suggestions in this chapter compare with present practice in your team or department?

- Have you identified any areas for improvement in the way you write care plans or complete individual service contracts?

- Are there any aspects of specifying individual care needs in which you would like further training or guidance?

This chapter has looked at the features of good service specifications and discussed how these principles can be applied in specifying individual care needs. In practice, many care plans are not clear specifications; they are simply statements about how much service will be provided or what time someone will call. Sometimes users are not even shown the individual service contract or given a copy of the care plan. This is unsatisfactory in terms of both professional and business practice.

Not all the ideas in this chapter will be relevant to care management arrangements in your local authority, but you may feel that some could be usefully adopted or adapted in your own practice. You may find it useful to turn to Chapter 10 and make notes on topics you would like to know more about as a result of working through this chapter. Talk to your line manager about any training needs you have identified.

RECOMMENDED READING

- *Assessing Needs and Planning Care in Social Work* (1993) Brian Taylor and Toni Devine, Arena. See Chapter 3 'Care planning' for a broader discussion about defining aims and objectives in social work and care planning.

- *Guidance on Contracting for Domiciliary and Day Care Services* (1995) Association of Metropolitan Authorities, Association of County Councils and Association of Directors of Social Services, published by Local Government Management Board. See particularly the sections on 'Guidance on Individual Service Contract' and 'Service Specification'.

- *Purchase of Service: Practice Guidance and practice material for social services departments and other agencies* (1991) Department of Health Social Services Inspectorate, HMSO. See Chapter 3 'Service specification'.

- *Social Work and Community Care* (1995) Malcolm Payne, Macmillan. See Chapter 5 'Care planning' and Chapter 6 'Implementing care plans' for a useful review of research and good practice in care planning.

6 Ensuring quality

If you are involved in care management, you need to be able to analyse the quality of care management as a service in itself, and to analyse the quality of individual care provided to service users.

The aim of this chapter is to provide an introduction to the subject of quality, and the purpose of monitoring in care management. The first part of the chapter explores what is meant by quality, efficiency and effectiveness. It discusses how this is relevant not just to senior management but also to front-line workers. The second part looks at three approaches to quality used in business. The final part discusses what you can do within your own sphere of influence to promote and develop quality.

Although there may be a relationship between the quality and the price of a service, business approaches to quality management aim to find creative ways of improving quality at any given level of resources. Many practitioners would argue, however, that the level of resources ultimately limits the quality that can be achieved. This is a tension that all social services departments have to work with.

QUESTIONS THIS CHAPTER WILL TRY TO ANSWER

- What does 'ensuring quality' mean?
- What is the difference between efficiency and effectiveness?
- Why is it helpful to understand inputs, activities, outputs and outcomes in order to analyse quality?
- What is the difference between quality control, quality assurance and total quality management?
- What is the role of care management in ensuring quality?

WHAT DOES
'ENSURING QUALITY' MEAN?

A key aspect of the Government's community care policy changes is the emphasis on ensuring the quality of services.

> A critical issue in commissioning care services will be the establishment of quality standards which meet the requirements of the purchaser [and] service user and to which the service provider is committed.
>
> *Policy Guidance*, para 4.18

To drive this forward, the Government has required local authorities and health and housing authorities to publish local community care charters from April 1996. The charters should include information about the specific quality standards to which community care services will be delivered and monitored.

Guidance on the purchase of services identifies the ideological background to these changes.

> In the last decade central government policy has placed great emphasis on the need for the efficient use of available resources in the public sector. Efforts have been directed to introducing managerial approaches and cultural attitudes found in the private sector. Consequently the White Paper [*Caring for People*] places emphasis on the rights of service users as customers and the need for services to be more responsive to their needs.
>
> *Purchase of Service*, para 5.1.3

Guidance also refers to quality approaches developed for industry and the commercial services. It acknowledges that there may be some difficulties in applying these quality approaches to the caring services but regards them as 'transferable and useful' (*Purchase of Service*, para 5.1.5). One basic principle is that quality is never achieved by accident but is the result of deliberate and systematic actions to achieve quality: 'Quality cannot be "inspected into" a product or service as an afterthought. It must be designed and built in as an integral part of service development ...' (*Purchase of Service*, para 5.1.5).

We can draw a number of guiding principles from the Government guidance on purchasing services, and we will explore these in the following sections:

- the need to use public resources efficiently;
- the emphasis on the rights and needs of service users;
- the use of quality approaches adapted from industry and commerce;
- the need for service quality standards and appropriate monitoring procedures;
- the need to design quality into services from the beginning;
- the requirement that service providers are committed to quality.

EFFICIENT USE OF RESOURCES

The efficient use of resources is of concern to everyone involved in caring organisations. When limited resources are used inefficiently, this could mean that the volume of needs being met isn't as great as it could be. It could also mean that the wrong needs are being met, so that lesser needs are catered for while more important ones are overlooked.

Deciding what is an efficient use of resources is not always straightforward. While a full discussion of efficiency is beyond the scope of this chapter, some analysis can help us to understand organisational attempts to improve efficiency and clarify our ideas about quality. The discussion which follows can be applied to the efficiency of independent service providers but equally to social services departments and care management staff.

To make meaningful statements about the efficiency of an organisation, department or team, we need to be able to:

- state clearly the objectives of the organisation;
- measure whether these objectives are being achieved;
- make valid comparisons with other organisations or delivery methods that achieve the same or similar objectives.

Being busy or achieving results?

A common problem for organisations trying to monitor efficiency is that they measure what can be measured rather than what matters. What matters is to measure those activities that fulfil the objectives (provided, of course, that the organisation's objectives are appropriately centred on the end user). In caring agencies, it is not the provision of a particular service that is the objective but enhancement of the quality of life for service users. A provider might produce excellent performance figures based on the number of hours of home care supplied that bore little relation to improvement in users' quality of life. This highlights the important distinction between efficiency and effectiveness. Efficiency refers to the output you get for given inputs. Effectiveness measures outcomes. The ideal, of course, is to be effective in an efficient manner.

In stating the objectives of an organisation it is important to state all of them, especially those that impose constraints on other objectives. Meeting users' needs and staying within budget, for example, are both aims of social services departments. Where conflicts like these arise and are identified, it is possible to devise strategies to deal with them. Where the tensions between objectives are not made explicit, they undermine the activities of the organisation and weaken any measures designed to evaluate effectiveness.

Another point to consider is how well the objectives match the needs and wants of the users of the service. A providing agency could be extremely effective in achieving its own objectives but if no one wants to use the service it provides, the contribution to quality is nil. This is discussed more fully below.

When comparing services and organisations, care needs to be taken that the comparisons are meaningful. This is particularly relevant in the caring services where personal interaction forms an important part of many services. Two home care providers may, for example, provide similar-looking services but one tries to ensure that the service is always provided by the same care worker while the other does not. Where there is consistency of staff, there is more opportunity for a personal relationship to develop between provider and user, and to fine-tune the service over time. Where staff change frequently, personal relationships and closely tailored services are less possible.

Whenever you come across measures that are supposed to tell you about the performance of a provider or service (quality standards, codes of practice, performance measures, performance indicators), ask yourself:

- What are the objectives of the service?
- Do the measures tell you how well the objectives are being achieved?
- Are you comparing like with like?

Analysing inputs, activities, outputs and outcomes

Another useful way of looking at your own service or the services you purchase is to look at the quality of the service process *as a whole*. This uses the same model that we saw in Chapter 5, looking at the service in terms of inputs, activities, outputs and outcomes. This model usefully focuses attention on outcomes as the final goal of the process. Too often standards are restricted to inputs, activities and outputs rather than the benefits or non-benefits to the user – the outcomes (in other words, they are about being busy rather than about doing things well and achieving results). As we shall see later, focusing on meeting users' needs appropriately is the lynchpin of well-designed quality systems.

Inputs are the resources used to deliver a service: people, money, materials, equipment, buildings, land, etc.

Activities, also called processes, are what we do with these inputs to produce what we want.

Outputs are what we produce as a result of our activities: either a tangible product or a less tangible service. Efficiency is concerned with how well the activities transform inputs into outputs.

Outcomes are the changes that the outputs bring about. In the caring services they are often less tangible than outputs: a typical outcome would be a specific improvement in the quality of life of the service user.

Outcomes are often less controllable than outputs. You can directly alter the flow of outputs by altering the inputs or the activities (reducing funding for a day centre reduces the number of places it can provide), but it is often difficult to know exactly what effects outputs have on outcomes (how do you measure the specific effects of respite care on the user's quality of life?).

The model helps us to look carefully at outcomes and the contribution of each stage to the outcomes:

- Do the outcomes meet the service user's needs appropriately?

- Do the outputs achieve desired outcomes – does transporting Nathaniel to a day centre, where he sits on his own most of the day, improve his quality of life?

- Are the activities consistent with desired outcomes – do review procedures based on written questionnaires completed by the service user yield the same quality of information as face-to-face interviews in the user's home?

- Are the inputs consistent with the desired outcomes – are staff trained to an adequate level?

It is also useful to ask how the desired outcomes compare with the objectives of the service, and how both compare with users' wants as well as their needs.

KEY APPROACHES TO QUALITY

Three approaches to quality developed in the commercial world are relevant to promoting quality in the caring services. They are:

- quality control
- quality assurance
- total quality management

Quality control

This involves a backwards look at quality. It assesses whether identified standards have been met in the provision of goods or services. It depends on systematic monitoring of the service by a variety of means, such as:

- performance indicators;
- monitoring of standards;
- regular quality audits and one-off quality audits;
- customer surveys;
- complaints procedures;
- self-evaluation by the provider – such as annual reports;
- regular reviews of users' progress and of service provision;

- other means of inspection to establish whether agreed quality standards have been met.

Contracts generally require service providers to monitor and report on the services that they provide. Purchasers, too, often carry out their own monitoring of services. The value of a monitoring system depends on what is being measured, how relevant this is to achieving the desired outcomes and an intelligent analysis of the results.

Care management staff have an important role in this process. Your access to informal feedback through daily contacts with service users, service providers and other professionals yields information not available through more formal methods of monitoring. It is important that good communication channels exist within the social services department to feed this information into the monitoring and evaluation process. This informal feedback helps to provide the context for interpreting other data. It contributes greatly to the balance of any conclusions drawn about the quality of a service.

CHECK YOUR OWN PRACTICE

- Are there clear mechanisms for feeding information acquired through informal means into the monitoring process in your department?
- Do you use this information in your review procedures?
- Is there any way of incorporating this information into the monitoring process between reviews?

Quality assurance

This is a proactive way of ensuring quality by designing a service to ensure that quality standards are always met. This means designing work processes to achieve a specified standard from the start and building in monitoring mechanisms to ensure that the specified standards are adhered to. Quality control is therefore an element in quality assurance, but whereas quality control looks backwards, quality assurance looks to the present and the future, to guarantee the quality of the outputs. It is based on the idea that it is cheaper to get things right first time rather than having to correct them later, and that quality has to be systematically pursued.

The elements of a quality assurance system are:

- a statement of policy identifying the quality standards which will be met;
- a system designed to ensure that these standards are met in all foreseeable circumstances;
- methods of verification, or checking, including quality control;
- formal feedback procedures on the operation of the system.

You may come across providers who operate a British Standard quality assurance system. This means that they have applied for (and received) external accreditation of their quality assurance system under BS5750/IS9000. There is, however, some criticism that these qualifications are primarily concerned with evaluating the systems that ensure the standards rather than the standards themselves.

The relevance of standards to the needs of the user is obviously critical in quality assurance systems. Where local authorities operate accreditation systems for approved providers, social services departments often require service specifications to be incorporated into the providers' quality assurance systems. Where this happens, it is particularly important that the views of service users and front-line workers, such as care managers, help to form the service specification. Standards can guarantee quality only when:

- The service meets the specified standard.
- The specified standard provides the service that users need.

If you have a choice of service providers, choosing those who operate quality assurance systems can provide some guarantee that standards will be met. Even so, you should always ask yourself about a provider:

- What standards are guaranteed? Are they so low that they actually reduce the desired quality of service?
- Do the standards meet the needs and wants of service users? Do they meet the standards of your department?
- Do the delivery systems meet the needs and wants of service users?
- Do the verifying systems actually test how well the standards are being met?
- Do the feedback mechanisms stimulate improvement in the quality of service?

Total quality management (TQM)

TQM means the total commitment of an organisation to quality; quality is defined in terms of meeting the customer's needs and wants. It requires that the whole culture of an organisation and all the people who work in it be dedicated to constant improvement in quality. TQM makes use of quality control and quality assurance in its search for all-embracing quality but it goes much further. Key features of TQM are:

The continual search to improve quality and the idea of incremental improvement (ie there should be 1 per cent improvement in quality 100 per cent of the time).

The recognition that quality is dynamic – today's quality achievements form tomorrow's minimum standards. Users always expect something better.

The commitment of every employee to quality – the role of management is to support front-line workers in achieving quality. Where there are problems, it is not because the people are wrong but because the system is wrong. Management's job is to provide the training, resources and work organisation that enable people to perform to their best.

The use of cooperative forms of working based on teams that constantly review and extend their own quality achievements.

Examination of every factor in the production of the service in terms of how it contributes to user satisfaction. Suppliers need to be brought into the quality system, as do methods of delivery and communication channels. Suppliers will be expected to meet specific standards.

The idea of the 'internal customer' The different parts of an organisation are all involved in supplier–customer relationships. It is the job of the suppliers to hone their products to meet the needs of their internal customers. Within each part of the organisation the same process is repeated: work teams doing different tasks relate to each other as suppliers and customers. The sum effect of this will be to transmit the needs of the external customer throughout the whole organisation.

TQM originated in industry and needs adapting to the social care context. However, ideas such as that of the internal customer give a useful stimulus when looking at the quality of service provided by social services departments, by strategic purchasing managers and care management staff, and by the independent providers who supply them with services.

TQM cannot be installed at an individual level: it requires the commitment of the whole organisation. Even where it is not adopted wholesale, elements of it can be used in discussions about quality within a particular part of a service, for example in an area office or team. The following statements could all provide a useful focus for discussion:

- Quality is defined by the user.
- Users' expectations of quality increase all the time.
- Quality is achieved by small improvements in quality all the time.
- The job of management is to support front-line workers in the pursuit of quality.
- Communicating information about a service is as much a question of quality as the service itself.

CHECK YOUR OWN PRACTICE

- Who is your customer? Is it your line manager, the service user, the local authority, the Government, the community at large or all of these?
- When you complete an assessment form, costing for a care plan, review or other paperwork, do you do it in such a way as to maximise the usefulness to your internal customers – the people who are going to make use of the information that you provide?
- Do you know how they will use the information, and in what form it is most helpful?

CARE MANAGEMENT AND QUALITY

Guidance on purchasing identifies four stages at which quality needs to be considered:

- drawing up the service specification;
- selecting potential or actual suppliers;
- drawing up the contract;
- monitoring the contract (*Purchase of Service*, para 5.2.1).

Although the design and implementation of quality management systems are not usually the responsibility of care management staff, the views of experienced front-line workers are an important input at each of these stages.

At the service specification stage, care management staff are able to provide current, well-informed and broadly based assessments of users' needs and acceptable ways of meeting them. Over time, you are likely to have practical day-to-day experience of the actual performance of different providers and of service components that are effective and give real satisfaction to service users. This practical experience will not be accessible to senior management unless there are effective channels to communicate it.

Care management staff can also contribute to the quality of the conditions section of the contract. Details such as purchasing arrangements, variation procedures, methods for resolving problems or disputes, appropriate liaison officers, subcontracting terms, complaints procedures and review procedures all benefit from practitioners' working knowledge of service provision. (See Chapter 4 for more about contract conditions.)

This working knowledge is equally valuable in identifying relevant performance indicators and meaningful monitoring systems. As we have noted, there is a tendency for management to select 'being busy' indicators that are easily measured rather than indicators that actually say something about the performance of the service. It is equally important that monitoring and review systems actually work in everyday working conditions. Elaborate systems that require a large time commitment are likely to get ignored when care workers are under pressure. Taking account during the design stage of the views of those who are going to work the system greatly improves its chances of working well.

WHAT YOU CAN DO TO PROMOTE QUALITY

In working with colleagues

- Use the supplier–customer model to analyse the services you provide to your colleagues. What are their needs? Do you meet them? Equally, what are your needs? Do your colleagues meet them?
- Do you communicate effectively with your colleagues and other professionals?

In working with clients

■ Do you constantly attempt to refine your understanding of service users' needs and wants? In assessment and care planning, do you define their needs in terms of outputs or outcomes?

■ Do you communicate effectively with service users, carers and other professionals involved in assessment and care planning? Do you clearly communicate your department's quality standards and complaints procedure to service users?

■ Do you select providers so as to obtain the closest fit between individual users' needs and the service? Do you take care to specify accurately individual care needs in the care plan and individual service contract?

■ Do you take care to analyse the **functional quality of services** – in other words, does the service satisfactorily carry out the identified tasks?

■ Do you analyse the **delivery quality of services** – is the service provided in a way that is considerate of the user's dignity, individuality and specific needs? Is it performed in the way that the user wants?

■ Do you systematically carry out monitoring and review procedures to verify that services are provided to standard, and to identify opportunities for further refinements to the service? Do you incorporate informal information from users, carers and providers into the monitoring and review process?

In working with service providers

■ Do you communicate the requirements of your client and your department to providers effectively?

■ Do you attempt to cooperate with them in raising standards?

■ Do you process their invoices promptly as part of your quality standards?

■ Do you try to work in partnership with them?

■ Do you see them as part of your quality management system?

If your social services department is developing or operating a quality assurance system, the ideas in this chapter may already be familiar to you, or they may have raised questions that you can answer only by finding out more about how your local system operates. There may be a quality assurance officer who can provide further information and/or training.

If your authority has not yet developed internal quality assurance systems for community care and care management, there may still be opportunities within your locality or team to adopt or adapt some of the features discussed in this chapter. Talk to your line manager if you feel that discussion would be helpful.

The action plan in Chapter 10 provides space for you to make notes on any questions or issues that you would like to follow up from this chapter.

RECOMMENDED READING

- *Managing Quality of Service* (1995) Alan Lawrie, Directory of Social Change. This easy-to-read guide is written mainly for voluntary organisations, but it explains the general principles of quality systems in terms that are accessible and useful for care management staff.

- *Quality in Public Services* (1995) Lucy Gaster, Open University Press. Useful general discussion of how the principles of quality assurance can be applied in the public services.

Official guidance referred to in this chapter

- *Community Care in the Next Decade and Beyond. Policy Guidance* (1990) HMSO.

- *Purchase of Service. Practice Guidance and practice material for social services departments and other agencies* (1991) Department of Health Social Services Inspectorate, HMSO. See Chapter 5 'Quality assurance in purchase of service'.

7 Financial skills

This chapter looks at money matters. It discusses the basic understanding and skills that front-line workers need to purchase services for users. The first part of the chapter introduces budgets, their purpose and how they are used to purchase community care services. A key element in the community care reforms is the use of devolved (or delegated) budgets (see pp 43–44). Some local authorities have moved in this direction more rapidly than others. In some authorities, care managers have their own budgets and purchase services from both in-house and external providers. But at present the majority of care management staff do not hold their own budgets. This chapter assumes that you are required to submit costings to a budget-holder for approval.

The middle part of the chapter sets out general principles to help you make the best use of the budgets available to you, to cost care packages and to present your costings to the budget-holder for approval. The last section looks at the final part of the equation in purchasing care services: what money users contribute to pay for the care they receive, and how you can help people who need care to make the most of their own financial resources.

QUESTIONS THIS CHAPTER WILL TRY TO ANSWER

- Why does the Government wish to see budgets devolved to care management level?
- How can front-line workers make the most effective use of the budgets available to them?
- How can you help service users get the most out of their own financial resources?

UNDERSTANDING BUDGETS

This section discusses the purpose of budgets, where the money for community care comes from, and how budgets are used to purchase community care services.

What is a budget?

A budget is first and foremost a plan, which shows the resources needed (money, people, skill mix, buildings, equipment) and how they will be used in the coming year. (Many budgets are presented simply as estimates of income and expenditure.) No two social services departments divide their budgets in the same way, so you will need to find out more about your own authority's financial structure from your budget-holder, or from the relevant finance or accounting officer.

In most social services departments, budgets for purchasing community care services are held at the level of first or second line manager. This is the level of budget that is relevant to care management; for the purposes of this chapter, this is what is meant when 'the budget' is referred to.

Like all budgets, the budget from which you buy community care services for users has several purposes:

- It reflects the social services department's objectives and priorities for community care.
- It is a plan of the year's work.
- It is a forecast of the year's expected income and spending.
- It is a tool for controlling and measuring results.

When the budget-holder to whom you are accountable prepares the budget for the coming year, it generally covers four broad areas of information:

- predicted costs for the year;
- outputs (for example number of residential and nursing home placements, total hours of domiciliary, day or respite care to be purchased, etc);
- anticipated income for the year;

- supplementary information (for example last year's budget for comparison, explanatory notes such as 'costs will be higher in May owing to relocation of residents from bankrupt home', etc).

Moving goalposts?

A budget is a plan for the future, but the future is always uncertain. There are many unknowns which can result in actual costs and outputs at the end of the year looking quite different from those in the original budget. These may be **external factors** such as changes in Government policy, cuts in Government funding, a very severe winter or a provider going bankrupt, or **internal factors** such as changes in service priorities or purchasing arrangements. Finally, the development of the mixed economy of care means that, since 1993, budgets have had to predict the cost of arranging services in a new way, often using new and untried providers. The costs of doing new things are always harder to predict with accuracy.

These are some of the reasons why users, providers and care management staff inevitably feel at times that the goalposts of community care budgets are constantly shifting. As the reformed system settles down, experience will enable social services departments and community care budget-holders within those departments to predict the following year's spending needs with more accuracy. But there are always likely to be unforeseen events during the year which alter the actual amount of resources available, and the volume or range of services you are able to purchase from month to month.

WHERE COMMUNITY CARE MONEY COMES FROM

Local authorities
Local authorities have always spent considerable amounts on directly provided community care services such as residential care, home care, day care and respite care, as well as on retirement housing and grants for adaptations and improvements provided by housing authorities. Local authority money for community care comes from a variety of sources.

The revenue support grant and standard spending assessment
The largest part of a local authority's grant from central government comes through the **revenue support grant:** money raised from national taxation which is given to local authorities to run the services which they are by law required or enabled to provide.

The Government decides how much it thinks each local authority ought to spend to provide a standard level of services – this is called the **standard spending assessment**. Figures such as the proportion of older people in the population are taken into account when calculating the standard spending assessment for an authority.

Special Transitional Grant (STG)
Each year from 1993–94 to 1996–97 the Government has transferred to local authorities money which it calculates that the Department of Social Security would have used to pay for care in homes under the old system (the 'transfer element'; see p 22), plus money for development and implementation costs, plus money to administer the Independent Living Fund. This Special Transitional Grant is 'ring-fenced' for community care services (which means that the money cannot be spent on other local authority services). In England, 85 per cent of the transfer element of the STG has to be spent in the independent sector. Each year, the amount of last year's STG is added to the local authority's standard spending assessment and is no longer ring-fenced.

Specific grants
The NHS and Community Care Act 1990 created 'specific grants' – ring-fenced money which can be spent only on new services for certain client groups or particular tasks. At present, the grants available will support up to 70 per cent of the total spending (the authority must provide the rest) for these purposes: mental illness, HIV and AIDS, alcohol and drugs, training and (for children) guardians ad litem and reporting officers. Spending these grants does not count towards meeting the requirement to spend 85 per cent of the transfer element of the STG in the independent sector.

Council Tax
Each local authority raises some of its funds through the Council Tax. In recent years the Government has 'capped' or put limits on the amount of money local authorities can raise in this way.

Fees for services
Social services departments raise money through fees which they can charge for certain services. For example, they can charge for meals on wheels, home care, day care and respite care, but they cannot charge for social work or care management services. The Government assumes that 9 per cent of the funds needed for domiciliary and day care services provided by the local authority will come from charges to users.

Health care
Funds for hospital and community health care come from the purchasing budgets of health authorities and fundholding GPs. They cannot charge individuals for hospital and community health services. Although the local authority is responsible for arranging community care services, the availability of local hospital and community health services is outside its control.

This has created difficulties in some areas; to encourage all the services involved in community care to work more closely with each other, the Department of Health published practical guidance on joint commissioning in 1995. In early 1995, the Government also directed health authorities to decide on eligibility criteria and the pattern and level of services for continuing health care needs for their area by April 1996.

Housing and housing services

The living conditions of people who need care are as important to their quality of life as the care services they receive. Housing for rent is provided mainly by local authorities and housing associations. Both are funded partly by central government. Money for housing associations is allocated by the Housing Corporation, which was set up to fund and monitor their work. Housing associations must raise money from the private sector to build new properties.

Most local authority housing money goes towards maintaining and repairing existing housing. They can give grants for repairs, improvements or adaptations to private owners, and in some cases to private tenants. The Government has cut expenditure on housing in recent years: for example, it has reduced the money available for disabled facilities grants.

Individuals' money

Much of the money to pay for community care comes directly from the people who need care, their carers and families. This money includes their own income and savings, social security benefits and, in some cases, for people needing residential or nursing home care, cash realised from the sale of their home.

Source Adapted from *The Community Care Handbook* (1995).

THE REASON FOR DEVOLVED BUDGETS

To meet the Government's objectives of developing needs-led services and promoting a flourishing independent sector, social services budgets must be redirected away from historical patterns of service delivery. It is the Government's view that when resources are allocated centrally, social services departments tend to concentrate on the take-up of existing services. Delegating budgets to care management staff who are not involved in service provision is one way of separating decisions about what kind of care the user needs from the existing pattern of services (*Purchase of*

Service, para 2.4.5). The aim of devolved budgets is to put purchasing power as close as possible to the service user. It is the Government's view that if front-line workers have budgetary authority to purchase services, the result will be more responsive and innovative services, but this has yet to be fully evaluated.

The Government recognised that the results of devolved budgets might be unpredictable; guidance suggested that budgets should be devolved gradually, and only when the necessary training and support for the next level of budget-holding was in place (*Purchase of Service*, para 2.4.9). Delegating budgets also requires adequate information and monitoring systems, to keep track of how much is being spent, by whom and on what; setting up these systems takes time.

There are disadvantages in devolving budgets. If this happens too fast, without the development of adequate planning and support systems, the purchasing activity of front-line workers can skew the pattern of providers in unpredictable ways (see p 47). It can become more difficult for a local authority to make strategic plans for service development and to 'manage the market' (encourage the range and type of independent providers that the authority requires) (*Care Management and Assessment, Managers' Guide*, paras 1.16–21).

If front-line workers have responsibility for allocating resources, this changes the nature of their relationship with service users. They are inevitably less able to act as advocates on users' behalf (see pp 29–30). Some authorities have therefore been slower in devolving budgets than others.

MAKING GOOD USE OF THE BUDGET

Social care manager: 'I never thought when I finished my training that I would end up haggling on the telephone with providers, or arguing with my boss about whether the cost of a service was really justified. I wanted to help people, not argue over money.'

This section looks at the financial questions you need to consider when costing a care plan, and at how to present your costing and increase your chances of getting it approved by the budget-holder. Care packages must be needs-led (ie based on assessment of need matched against eligibility criteria), but budget managers also expect them to be cost-effective. These are key questions that you will need to consider before finalising the care plan:

- How much flexibility are you allowed in buying services? Are you well informed about policies and procedures which determine the maximum weekly costs of care packages? Do you need special authorisation to spend above a certain weekly level?

- Are you well informed about eligibility criteria?

- Will the budget-holder automatically approve certain needs but not others?

- What type of contract can/should you use? Is there guidance on when you should use a block or spot contract? (See pp 77–79 for more information about types of contract.)

- Have you got enough information to compare the cost and quality of different providers/services?

- Does the user require the service on a long-term basis? Is the user's condition likely to remain the same, get better or get worse?

- What will the cost to the user be? Is the user able/willing to pay the charges for the different options you are considering? Has the user's eligibility for welfare benefits been checked? (See the information on charging policy on pp 132–133.)

- If the cost of the care package is likely to be high, does the user qualify for help from the Independent Living Fund?

- Are you well informed about any other special budgets which you may be able to draw on for certain kinds of need?

Practice varies widely. Some authorities impose a cash limit on care packages for people living at home, typically around the cost of equivalent care in a residential or nursing home. At present, other authorities are moving in this direction but do not formally impose a limit. Some authorities have lower maximum spending limits for older people than for younger people. (This is not sound practice as it discriminates against older people.)

You need to be well informed and up to date about available budgets, eligibility criteria and charging policy. As we saw on page 119, resources can change during the year for many different reasons. If, for example, fewer people than expected need residential care in the first half of the year, more money may be available to purchase other services in the second half. Eligibility criteria can also be narrowed or broadened as a way of controlling costs. For historical reasons, there may be a separate budget for certain specialised needs. If you are to make the best use of budgets available to you, your budget-holder should keep you well informed. Raise this issue if you feel that communication about budgets is not as good as it should be. (See also pp 128–129 on working with the budget-holder.)

COSTING THE CARE PACKAGE

Below is an example of a costed care package.

Mrs Martin is a widow, aged 67, on Income Support. She is partially sighted, has severe arthritis, and can only walk short distances with the aid of a stick. Mrs Martin has recently had a bad fall but wishes to remain as independent as possible. Her daughter lives locally but has a full-time job. She calls in daily to make an evening meal and help her mother into bed, and looks after her at weekends. After discussion between Mrs Martin, her daughter and the care manager, the agreed care plan includes day care, home care including help with getting up and preparing a midday meal, a community alarm, and respite care to give her daughter a break.

THE COST OF MRS MARTIN'S CARE PACKAGE

Service	Unit cost	Unit	Frequency	Weekly cost
Home care (directly provided) 3 hours × 3 days per week	no cost	per hour	3	–
Getting up service (private agency) 1 hour × 5 days per week	£5.50	per hour	5	£27.50
Day centre (voluntary organisation) 2 days per week	£32.00	per day	2	£64.00
Community alarm service (private agency)	£6.50	per week	1	£6.50
Total				£98.00

Respite care approximately every 12 weeks at £290 per week.

In the medium term, Mrs Martin is likely to need a stair lift or downstairs toilet and washing facilities.

Mrs Martin's social services department requires care management staff to cost only services bought from independent providers. Directly provided services are paid for from a different budget. In some authorities, all services must be costed by the care manager.

Care packages are costed on a weekly basis. The unit cost of each service is multiplied by the number of times the service is provided each week. This gives a weekly cost for each service. These are then added together to give the total weekly cost of the care package. Additional costs (such as double time for bank holidays or weekends, and travel allowances) should be carefully checked and added into the daily or weekly total, as appropriate.

Costs that will arise at longer intervals than a week (for example respite care on a quarterly basis, or costs for a one-off service such as a major cleaning of someone's home) are usually shown separately. The budget-holder needs to know at what frequency they will occur, so that one-off, monthly or quarterly costs from all the care packages approved can be spread over the year in the budget.

Capital costs (for example for a stair lift) should also be shown separately. Capital costs are generally recorded under a separate heading in the budget. They also need to be spread over the year.

Working out the weekly costs of more complex care packages calls for accurate maths and can be very time-consuming. Using a calculator or learning to use a computer spreadsheet, if you have access to one in your office, can make this task a lot easier. Talk to your line manager about training if you have difficulty doing more complex calculations – many people do.

Tips for costing the care package

Work backwards from the outcomes specified in the care plan

If you start from the desired outcomes you have identified with the user, you can think flexibly about the inputs and activities needed to achieve them (see pp 99–100), and then compare the costs and quality of the options available.

Make sure that you are well informed about the wider goals, strategies and priorities that care packages should reflect

These may be in the form of written policy or guidance for your service, area or team; informal guidance from your line manager; or simply unwritten practice. Operational guidelines should in principle relate back to the community care plan, and local or national budgeting priorities. In 1995–96, for example, £30 million of the total Special Transitional Grant paid to local authorities was earmarked by the Government for the development of home care and respite care services. This might result in a social services department arranging a block contract for respite nursing care with two or three providers, and asking front-line workers to use those providers where feasible.

Balance the user's priorities with those of the budget-holder

Budget constraints mean that front-line workers have to plan care packages by balancing 'What is required?' with 'What is achievable?' You may be asked by the budget-holder to identify those care needs which it is 'essential' to meet and those which are 'desirable'. Users' views about what is essential or desirable vary according to personal preference and circumstances. Some users might give high priority to help with shopping and cooking, because they put a high value on being able to choose and prepare their own food. Others may prefer meals on wheels because it frees them from physically difficult tasks. Many older people who qualify for community care services live in poor housing needing repair and adaptation. Some may regard improvements to their living conditions as much more essential than a home care service.

Balance individual needs with average expectations

Ideally, you should be able to look at the nature of the tasks or activities needed to support the user, and then decide how many hours these will take; this is more realistic than simply costing in the standard or average number of hours available for that category of user. Many home care schemes have worked out standard times for certain tasks but it may, for example, take up to an hour to feed a person who has severe difficulty in swallowing, while another person may need less than half this time. A carer can give you a lot of information about the time needed for daily activities, but bear in mind that an agency care worker, who will at first be a stranger, may need much longer to complete these tasks than the carer does.

Spell out assumptions

Costing the care package is similar to preparing a larger budget, in that you are planning for uncertainty. If at the end of the year a care package that you devised has actually cost twice as much as you expected, your budget-holder will want to know why. If you know that the costs of a particular care package are likely to be unpredictable, spell this out in additional notes attached to your costing. This can help you to explain any difference between the costing and actual spending at the end of the year. It also helps your budget-holder.

> **Example:** The only agency providing night sitters in your area has from time to time proved unreliable, but recent action by the contracts manager is supposed to have sorted this out. 'The night-sitting costs are based on using . . . agency. Extra costs may be incurred if emergency cover has to be arranged with another agency, as has happened in the past.'

> **Example:** A new day centre run by a voluntary organisation is due to open in the user's area: 'This costing is based on the assumption that . . . Centre opens on schedule. Transport to . . . Centre (£ . . . per day) will be necessary otherwise.'

> **Example:** A service user recovering from a stroke is expected to regain mobility in his left leg in three months: 'It is expected that it will be possible to reduce the home care service from six to two hours per week after three months, but this depends on progress in recovering mobility.'

Allocate more time to the more expensive parts of the care package

Providing you remain within guidelines for costing care packages, it may be useful to think in terms of the major, significant and minor costs within the care package. Get in the habit of monitoring the time you spend on major and minor items. It makes sense to spend more time sourcing (finding, costing and checking the quality of) services or equipment that constitute the major part of the total cost. It doesn't make sense to spend a lot of time sourcing a minor service. The difference between two similar community alarm schemes, for example, may be 25 pence a week, or £13 a year. The difference in the charges of two home care agencies may add up to £40 per week, or around £2,000 a year. The quality of service provided by the more expensive agency may be worth more than the difference in cost, but it may not. It is clearly important to spend time on this major part of the service to the user.

WORKING WITH THE BUDGET-HOLDER

If you have to submit costed care plans to a budget-holder for approval, the suggestions below may be helpful. Even where there are tightly drawn guidelines for costing and approving care packages, budget-holders may have some leeway in how these are interpreted. Where guidelines are less tightly drawn, there is more scope for budget-holders to use their personal judgement about what costs are reasonable or unreasonable. One person may be prepared to spend up to the limits of their budget, or to exceed it if the reasons are good; another may feel it is essential to remain within budget, or even to underspend. Some budget-holders work in an open, straightforward way; some are less open. Recognise that you each have different roles: this is a tension which calls for negotiating skills.

- Get to know your budget-holder and understand how he or she assesses costings. Learn to recognise what is likely to be approved and what is not.

- Make sure the costing is well reasoned, informative and clearly set out.

- Provide additional notes where useful on the assumptions, reasons and calculations behind your costing (including risk assessment). Or keep a record of them.

- Be prepared to justify your costing; do this by presenting clear, objective arguments.

- Compare your financial costs with the social costs of *not* providing the service.

- If the budget-holder is not persuaded by your reasoned arguments, accept that you need to look for a compromise. Ask for advice on how you might modify the care package.

- If you are still concerned, ask for your views to be recorded, with any supporting evidence (for example a risk assessment).

Budget-holders often feel as much at the mercy of events outside their control as front-line workers do. What is important is that you and the budget-holder are able to work together to make maximum use of the resources that you can control. This is why it is important that budget-holders and care management staff communicate well with each other, sharing information and setting out assumptions. This can help to identify positive possibilities for change, as well as potential problems.

USERS' MONEY

Financial assessment

Assessment includes a review of the user's finances. Financial assessment has two objectives:

- to enable users to make the most of the financial resources that are available to them;
- to enable the local authority to calculate how much, if anything, users should pay towards the cost of the care services they receive.

Financial assessment is double-edged. On the one hand, users may find out from the assessment process that they can get a higher level of existing benefit, or additional benefits that they didn't know about. They may find out that they can realise income from pension or insurance schemes. On the other hand, they may be asked to put this additional income towards paying for services. If there is doubt, service users may need time to get independent financial advice from the Citizens Advice Bureau or other local welfare rights agency.

What is assessed?

Financial assessment procedures vary between authorities, so this section can give only a general guide: compare it with actual practice in your authority. The financial assessment system for residential and nursing home care is national, but financial assessment and charges for domiciliary and day care are determined by the local authority. The systems are fully explained in Age Concern England's Factsheet 10 *Local authority charging procedures for residential and nursing home care* and Factsheet 6 *Finding help at home.*

The financial assessment should assess only the service user's resources. It should not take into account the finances of a spouse (unless money is held in a joint account) or of anyone else in the household.

In some cases people may be asked to complete their own financial assessment forms. But forms are often complicated, and generally front-line workers help users and carers to fill them in, and verify information at the same time (for example by asking for sight of pay slips, savings books, etc). This information is then reviewed by financial staff, who calculate what charges the user will have to pay. The assessment is returned to the front-line worker, who can then explain it to the service user.

Be clear about how far you are competent to give advice on financial matters. Individuals may need independent advice to ensure that their financial assessment is fair. The Citizens Advice Bureau and other independent welfare rights schemes have specialised workers, and you should not hesitate to refer potential service users to them if you are in any doubt.

Financial assessment usually includes questions about:

Present income You may be required to ask the user for proof of recent earnings (recent payslips, or latest accounts if the person is self-employed).

Personal pensions Check whether the user is entitled to a waiver of contributions, or to an income or lump sum now, because of illness or disability. But do check that he or she will not receive a much smaller pension as a result of drawing it early.

Benefits claimed You may be required to ask for proof of benefits received, if certain benefits act as a 'passport' to free services from the local authority.

Insurance policies, for example to cover sickness, mortgage protection or loss of earnings because of sickness or disability (permanent health insurance). The user may be entitled to a waiver of contributions, or to income from the policy.

Income tax allowances The user and his or her spouse may not be getting the full allowances that they are entitled to. Refer them to their tax office or an independent advice agency.

How the illness or disability affects daily living activities – to help identify whether the user is entitled to benefits they are not already receiving.

Capital or savings – bank, building society or post office accounts; stocks and shares; National Savings certificates.

The assessment form should ask detailed questions about the user's expenditure, to make sure that calculations take into account everything that the user has to spend. This should include questions about:

Extra expenses because of illness or disability – for example extra heating costs, more expensive foods for a special diet, a special bed or other furniture, special equipment. (Sometimes these are described as 'abnormal' expenses on the assessment form; some users are put off by the term 'abnormal' and may need prompting to identify these extra expenses.)

Other outgoings Users may have significant expenses apart from those itemised on the assessment form, for example the cost of running a specially adapted car for someone with a disability; contribution to a son or daughter's childcare costs; taxis to visit a relative. Find out about these and note them down, even if you are not sure whether they will be taken into account.

If the user is being assessed for a residential or nursing home place, the value of any property may be counted as savings, so you will need to ask for information about:

- property or land in this country or abroad;
- mortgage or loans secured against these;
- current market value of the property;
- other people living in the user's house.

If certain other people live in the house, the local authority may not be able to count its value as savings. For more information on whether this applies to your client, see Age Concern England Factsheet 10 *Local authority charging procedures for residential and nursing home care.*

CHECK YOUR OWN PRACTICE

- How do the questions listed here compare with those on assessment forms used in your own authority?

- Do you know who to ask for advice if you or the user would like an explanation of the assessment calculations?

An officer who does the financial calculations may be able to provide training or visit service users to explain how these are worked out.

Helping users to make the best use of their own money

You may know from experience that going through the financial assessment form with users can be complicated and time-consuming. It is not surprising that charging policies and means-testing are contentious aspects of community care: financial assessment and its results often arouse strong feelings in users and carers.

Financial assessment can be made more productive for you and your clients if you can regard it not simply as a bureaucratic, administrative task but as an opportunity to explain the local authority's charging policies and procedures, to explore users' and carers' financial situation and possible sources of financial support, to give them clear information about their rights, and, where appropriate, to tell them about independent sources of advice. To do this you need to be well informed about the following:

Your local authority's charging policy

Users and carers are often given confusing and contradictory information by different staff. Try to provide clear information and sort out any confusions. (It is easier to accept a charging system which you consider unfair if you know that everyone is being treated equally unfairly.)

Anomalies in charging policy

Charging policies for day care and domiciliary services vary widely: what, if any, charges are made is a matter of local authority discretion. Some local authority charging procedures have been questioned as legally dubious. If there are areas of dispute within your own authority's policy, users who are likely to be affected should be told that they have the right to appeal against charges.

(There is not the space in this book to go into details about the many anomalies that have arisen with the reformed charging system. Age Concern England publishes a regularly updated factsheet on charging procedures for residential and nursing home care, and the local authority associations are at present drafting guidelines on charging policies for social services managers. The local authority welfare rights unit may be able to advise users if your care management responsibilities make it difficult for you to act as advocate on these issues.)

Health authority policy on who is eligible for NHS-funded continuing care

Paying for nursing home care may be the responsibility of the health authority (and so free to the user) or the local authority (and so means-tested): policies are locally agreed, so the boundaries of responsibility vary from area to area. You should be familiar with the eligibility criteria of any health authority that you deal with. (The relevant health authority is that which covers the patient's place of residence.) In some cases, users may have good grounds for asking for a review of a decision that they are not eligible for NHS funding. In-patients can use NHS appeal procedures, but after discharge the service user must use the social services complaints procedure.

Welfare benefits and sources of advice

The Disability Rights Handbook (updated annually) and the free Benefits Enquiry Line (0800 88 22 00) for people with disabilities and their carers are useful sources of information about benefits for front-line workers and service users.

Grants

Some users may not be aware that they could be eligible for a grant or small income from a professional association, trade union or armed forces charity. Charities concerned with a specific illness or condition may also give grants (for example the Cancer Relief Macmillan Fund). Consider asking for training in how to help community care users to obtain grant aid.

'The loophole'

At present, there is a legal loophole which enables people who go into residential or nursing home care to protect their home from being counted as capital (ie savings) while it is waiting to be sold. Some social services departments provide information for service users about this, but others do not. The local authority welfare rights unit, if there is one, or the Disability Living Allowance helpline (0345 123 456) can provide further information and advice for service users.

The social services department's complaints procedure and sources of independent financial advice

A user or carer can ask for a review of the financial assessment through the complaints procedure (informal and formal) if they believe that they have been wrongly assessed or unfairly charged for services. Users may ask you for advice about, for example, whether they should ask for a review of a decision, how they can limit their liability to pay charges, or whether they should cash in an insurance policy.

If there are no guidelines for front-line workers, get advice from your line manager, finance department or welfare rights unit about the limits of the financial advice you can give, and when you should direct users to independent sources of advice. Keep yourself well informed about which local agencies can offer reliable financial advice.

CHECK YOUR OWN PRACTICE

- Are you familiar with the local health authorities' eligibility criteria for nursing home care?
- How much do you know about helping community care users to obtain grants?
- Are you clear about when you can give users financial advice and when you should direct them to independent agencies?

This chapter has provided a basic introduction to some of the areas of financial knowledge and skills that you need to buy services for users. It is worth remembering that no one really likes handling budgets and costings: front-line workers often say that they find this one of the least satisfying aspects of care management. But developing skills to make the most of limited budgets, and to enable users to make the most of theirs, can help you make the reformed system work as far as possible *for* users and *not* against them.

You may want to note on the action plan in Chapter 10 any topics on which you would like further information or training.

RECOMMENDED READING

At present, there is very little material which deals specifically with financial skills for care management. You may find it useful to look at one of the many short introductory guides to business budgeting. Many of the principles can be applied to care management, especially if you hold your own budget. One example is:

- *Essentials of Business Budgeting* (1995) Robert G Finney, WorkSmart Series, Amacom, New York.

For general information on charging policies, see:

- *Advice Note on discretionary charges for adult services* (January 1994) Department of Health Social Services Inspectorate.

- *Commentary on Social Services Inspectorate Advice Note* (August 1994) Association of Metropolitan Authorities/Local Government Information Unit.

- Age Concern England Factsheet 10 *Local authority charging procedures for residential and nursing home care*. A general guide to charging procedures which is regularly updated. You may find it useful to compare this summary with practice in your own authority.

- *Charging Consumers for Social Services: Local authority policy and practice* (1995) National Consumer Council.

- *The Community Care Handbook: The reformed system explained* (1995) Barbara Meredith, ACE Books. Chapter 8 'Paying for care' provides a general outline of charging arrangements and some of the variations in policy and procedures between local authorities.

Official guidance referred to in this chapter

■ *Care Management and Assessment: Practitioners' Guide* (1991) Department of Health Social Services Inspectorate, Scottish Office Social Work Services Group, HMSO. Official guidance for practitioners.

■ Joint Circular HSG(95)8/LAC(95)5 *NHS Responsibilities for Meeting Continuing Health Care Needs.*

■ *Practical Guidance on Joint Commissioning* (1995) Department of Health.

8 Negotiating

Negotiating is an important part of care management. The aim of this chapter is to discuss different approaches to negotiating and to review the understanding and skills that can help you to be an effective negotiator.

The first part of the chapter sets out some common attitudes and approaches to negotiating, and discusses which of these are most relevant to care management. The second part concentrates on negotiating with providers, which is a relatively new activity for many front-line workers. The final part of the chapter looks at how to plan for negotiating, and describes some negotiating tactics to watch out for.

QUESTIONS THIS CHAPTER WILL TRY TO ANSWER

- Why are negotiating skills important for care management?
- What are the different approaches to negotiating? Which are most useful?
- What are the important stages in the negotiating process?
- What negotiating tactics are useful?

NEGOTIATING IN CARE MANAGEMENT

Negotiating is the process by which people with different viewpoints move to a point where they can reach agreement. Negotiating involves skills in communicating with other people similar to those used in traditional areas of social work such as counselling, groupwork, teamwork and arranging or coordinating services. Aspects of negotiating also have much in common with assertiveness training. All these activities involve interpersonal skills such as listening, using non-verbal communication, being aware of styles of communication (aggressive, open or manipulative) and an ability to see (while not necessarily agreeing with) the other person's point of view.

For front-line workers, assessing needs and buying care creates new situations where negotiating skills are important:

- assessing needs and preferences with users and carers;
- joint assessment and care planning with other professionals and agencies;
- getting approval of the care package from the budget-holder;
- negotiating the individual service contract and price with providers.

Negotiating skills are needed in each of these relationships. They are also needed to find a way through the differing and sometimes conflicting views of all these people, each of whom has a particular perception of the needs and outcomes that should shape the care package.

APPROACHES TO NEGOTIATING

The previous section began with a rather broad definition of negotiating, but there are many different ways of approaching negotiations. A brief review of the approaches most relevant to care management will be helpful.

'Helping' negotiation

Therapeutic social work (for example counselling and groupwork) involves negotiation, but in these situations the worker is there as a professional to help or advise other people. Objectively, the worker is in a position of control (however supportively this authority is exercised), so the relationship between the parties involved is an unequal one.

'Equal-position' negotiation

Arranging care in the community is much more about working with others as equals. The care management worker clearly does not control a substantial part of the resources that may be needed to support a user in the community. Buyers and suppliers come together on equal terms to negotiate a deal, at least in principle, and the front-line worker has to approach providers as co-professionals and equals. The same is true when negotiating with other professionals and agencies that are gate-keepers to resources, and with people who are part of the user's informal support network. The front-line worker cannot direct a carer to provide care.

There are different views about the most effective approach in equal-position negotiation.

Win–lose negotiation

This is a common approach in buying and selling negotiations, where the parties involved have conflicting needs. Each person aims to get the best possible outcome for themselves, without concern for the other. Any advantages gained by this sort of approach tend to be short term. The loser may not want to do business with the winner in future. This approach seems less appropriate where the quality of personal relationships is an essential part of what is being negotiated.

Win–win negotiation

This is based on the view that the simplest way to achieve agreement is to persuade the other person that giving you what you want will give them what they want too. In other words, there is concern for the other person's outcome as well as your own. This approach has advantages in the long term. If both sides can feel that they have gained advantages, future relationships are likely to be positive.

Joint problem-solving

If both parties share a high level of concern for their own and the other person's outcomes, the result tends to be cooperative rather than conflict-driven negotiation. Negotiating is then a process of sharing the problem, exploring possibilities, and finding a solution to which there can be a shared commitment. This 'human' approach to negotiating is perhaps the most appropriate for care management, but it cannot work unless both parties share a concern for the other's outcome.

It is useful to develop an awareness of the different approaches adopted by people with whom you negotiate, and to match your approach to theirs where this is helpful.

NEGOTIATING WITH PROVIDERS

Social welfare officer: 'I can think of two homes that are particularly good to deal with. They are open and straight dealing. They won't promise anything they can't do, but if they say they will do something, I know that they will. I wish everyone was like that.'

Care manager: 'Some providers are very shrewd. I've come away from a discussion feeling like I've been bounced into a decision, without time to think it through or check it out with my client. I know I've been manipulated, but it's knowing how to avoid it.'

Negotiating with budget-holders and with clients is not an entirely new process for front-line workers, although the negotiations have been given a different emphasis with the community care reforms. But negotiating the fine details of contracts and prices with providers is an entirely new activity, and one about which many practitioners feel less than confident.

The starting point for successful negotiation should be a willingness to understand the other person's viewpoint and to work together. Some providers approach negotiations in this way, but others take a more hard-nosed approach, which front-line workers often feel ill equipped to deal with. This section provides a brief summary of five common styles in business negotiation. An awareness of these different styles can help you to recognise what the other person is hoping to achieve, and to decide whether you want to respond with the same or a different style.

Compromise means meeting in the middle, and it seems a fair way to negotiate. The golden rules, if you are going to compromise, are not to do it too soon – don't be bounced into it straight away – and to be clear in your own mind how much you are prepared to give. Start from a more extreme position than your real one, then the compromise is likely to be closer to what you actually want.

Bargaining is giving and taking. If there are several issues to be agreed, make a concession in return for a concession from the other person. 'I know the service user would be willing to share a room, but only if you can offer a better price, to include the "extras" in your brochure.' Once again, don't start bargaining too soon. Studies have shown that the first person to give is likely to go on giving. If you do make a concession first, link it to getting one in return.

Coercion is using threats, backed by economic muscle, to get what you want. As a major purchaser of care services, the social services department can, in principle, use its economic power to push down providers' prices. 'If you can't provide the service at this price I/we won't buy from you now, or in the future.' Equally, if there is no choice of suppliers, a monopoly provider can push prices up. Veiled threats are better than crude ones: 'If *you* can't help me on the price, I may have to look at other options.' The disadvantage of coercion is that it can create resentment and permanently sour relations.

Emotion can be a powerful tool in negotiating. Negotiations can be frustrating, and feelings may run high. But people who are used to selling often use emotional ploys to manipulate potential buyers. 'I'm afraid we can't guarantee that we'll still have the place tomorrow. I'm sure your client doesn't want to have to go through any more messing about. If you can give me your decision today, I can promise you the place.' Don't let your own or the other person's emotions control the decisions you make.

Logic seems a common-sense tool in negotiating. It is difficult to find room for negotiation if you are presented with a detailed and well-argued set of reasons for the other person's position (for example an increase in price or a change in terms). It makes sense to prepare carefully the facts and arguments to back up your own position, but it is especially important when you know that the other person uses this approach. Asking for more information, without becoming nitpicking, may help you to find weaknesses in the other person's logic.

CHECK YOUR OWN PRACTICE

- Which of these styles have you met in providers (and others) with whom you negotiate?
- Are you aware of it when a particular style is used on you? How does it make you feel?
- Are you aware of using any of these styles on other people?

These styles of negotiating are needed in the business world, and providers that have been used to operating as businesses for some time are more likely to use such techniques in a deliberate way. But we all make use of them from time to time in our negotiations with other people. You may feel a strong personal preference for styles or techniques which involve building trust, working cooperatively and shared problem-solving, which are more in harmony with the values that underpin the provision of social care. 'Softer' negotiating styles are appropriate for providers (and others) who prefer to work in collaborative ways (for example voluntary organisations, providers with whom the social services department has a long-standing relationship, and perhaps smaller, less profit-oriented providers). The point is that 'softer' styles are not effective against someone with a 'win–lose' negotiating approach, who is determined to manipulate the outcome to their best advantage.

PHASES OF NEGOTIATING

This section looks at the different stages in the negotiating process. An understanding of these stages can help you to plan your own approach, control the discussion rather than be controlled, and actively move things forward to a positive conclusion. There are various ways of describing the process, depending on the approach to negotiating. Two approaches are described here: first, a business management approach, often used in commerce in buying and selling situations; second, a joint problem-solving approach, which is more in tune with the principles of social care, and which you may already use in working with users, carers and other professionals.

PHASES OF NEGOTIATION – BUSINESS MANAGEMENT APPROACH

Open

■ Establish relationships – be warm but firm.

■ Decide what to say about the user's requirements for services, without giving everything away – this shapes the provider's expectations.

■ Take control, tactfully.

Test

■ Test your assumptions about the provider.

■ Get information about the provider's position: look, listen, ask questions.

■ Assess the provider's level of interest.

■ Check how firm the provider is on key points.

■ Look for weak points and probe them.

Move

■ Be prepared to give ground, but slowly, and try to get the provider to move first.

■ Persuade the provider to move towards your view on a particular point.

■ Be prepared to make a concession in return – know the cost and keep it small.

■ Help the discussion to flow.

■ Look and listen for signs of movement in the provider's position.

■ Offer creative suggestions – don't expect the provider to do all the work.

■ Watch out for 'dirty tricks'.

Agree

■ Look and listen for signs that the provider wishes to conclude.

■ Decide when a workable agreement has been reached (this could be anything from a final offer to an agreement to adjourn because no progress has been made).

■ Control the conclusion, tactfully.

■ Summarise what has been agreed with the provider: get a verbal 'yes' to the summary, make notes, write a letter to confirm if appropriate.

■ Decide next step – action, or next meeting if the result was a deadlock.

Source Adapted from *It's a Deal* (1989) Paul Steele et al, McGraw Hill, p 66.

PHASES OF NEGOTIATION – JOINT PROBLEM-SOLVING APPROACH

Preparation tasks	Joint tasks
Make a summary of all the facts of the situation	*Describe the problem. Ask the other person if they see it in the same way. If not, ask them to describe how they see it. You will need to reach agreement before you go on*
Make a list of possible solutions, however unlikely some of them may seem	*Offer your own suggestions. Ask the other person for their suggested solutions*
List any obstacles to each solution you have suggested	*Tell the other person what obstacles you can see. Ask them to explain any obstacles you are not aware of*
Decide which solution seems most feasible	*Exchange ideas about which solution seems most feasible, and move towards a workable agreement*
Decide what concrete steps you can take to make progress towards the solution	*Discuss what steps you can both take. Summarise the action agreed. Confirm with the other person: make notes or write a letter if appropriate*

Think back to the last negotiations that you were involved in. Which description of the phases of negotiation is closest to what actually happened?

In any negotiation, you need to be clear about where the other person is starting from. Are they approaching things from a business or problem-solving point of view, or a mixture of both? This will help you to organise your own moves accordingly.

Preparation

If you prepare and plan, you will be in a stronger negotiating position than if you don't. Prepare by researching:

What is required Know exactly what services you want to buy and in what quantity.

Your room for manoeuvre Know the exact limits beyond which you cannot move.

The state of the market Find out what other providers are available, their prices, how much they can supply, at what quality and when. Find out if there is surplus capacity in the market (more places than users) or excess demand (more users than places). What are the likely future developments in the market?

The costs of the provider If you can get an accurate idea of a provider's costs, you will be in a much stronger position to know whether the price quoted is fair or over-inflated. Find out costs from your contracts department, from other similar providers, or by adding up items like wages, equipment costs, and so on.

The strengths and weaknesses of the provider you are negotiating with.

What the provider is likely to want What might they ideally hope to achieve, and what is the minimum that they would accept?

Planning

Plan what you are going to do in each of the phases of negotiation described above. The overall aim of planning is to set the agenda for the meeting tactfully and to reduce the other party's expectations. Set a target range for yourself that you are willing to negotiate in, and specify this range precisely in terms of figures and services so that you can assess how successful you have been in your negotiations.

Make sure that you have worked out before the negotiations how much different options will cost and whether you can afford them. Take this list into the meeting: it's easy to miscalculate in the heat of a meeting. Do not base your assumptions on past pricing patterns: try instead to base them on your knowledge of costs.

HINTS FOR EFFECTIVE NEGOTIATION

- Find out about areas of mutual interest between you and the provider and use these to establish a rapport between you during the negotiating.

- Try to be as flexible as possible in thinking through different options beforehand. During negotiations, be prepared to be flexible in the order that you discuss things but have a list of the items that you intend to cover and make sure that they are all dealt with.

- Make sure that you are absolutely clear in your own mind what you want before you go into the negotiations. Be optimistic in your aims but keep them within the bounds of reason.

- On key items, state early in the discussion what your position is and stick closely to it.

- Do not compromise early in the meeting.

- Where you do bargain or compromise, do it on non-central issues, do it slowly, and always get something in return.

- Listen rather than talk, and listen to what is not said as well as what is said. Anything other than a bald statement of what is on offer allows room for negotiating.

- As each item is agreed, summarise the agreement verbally and write it down. At the end of the meeting, write up your own summary of what has been agreed and send a copy to the other party.

- If you know that you really need more time or more information before you can make a decision, be firm about adjourning the discussion. Never let the other party pressure you into an agreement against your better judgement.

Negotiating ploys

You may not wish to use these ploys yourself, but you should be aware that some experienced negotiators use such tactics to manipulate the discussion. Watch out for them, and know how to deal with them. Aim to be polite, firm and fair.

Emotional appeal 'I've got dreadful flu' or 'We've got terrible problems' might be an attempt to gain your sympathy in order to prevent you putting your case vigorously. Express sympathy but don't feel guilty or let it cloud your rational judgement.

Linking unrelated issues – tying issues together that are unrelated in an attempt to gain concessions. Sometimes negotiators will try to link agreement on a minor point to a broader agreement, implying that the larger deal will fail if they do not get what they want on the minor issue.

Broken record – repeating a position or demand over and over again until you give in out of exasperation. Respond with a polite reminder that you cannot agree to what is wanted, and firmly open up a new area for discussion.

The offer that is too good to refuse These offers should be treated with a great deal of suspicion: they are made because they benefit the other party.

Silence If one of your questions or proposals is met with silence, this may be to make you feel uncomfortable and encourage you to say (and give) more. Don't fall into the trap of trying to fill the silence by providing your own answers or making a concession. Stay silent yourself or ask the other person what they are thinking.

Physical discomfort Making you wait, giving you an uncomfortable chair or invading your body space can be done deliberately to make you feel uncomfortable. Be frank about what makes you feel uncomfortable and ask the other party to do something about it.

'I'll have to refer to . . . ' Try to establish before any negotiation that the person you are speaking to is empowered to make the decision or agree the deal. Otherwise this ploy allows the whole negotiation to be reopened.

Future promise 'If we can just do this deal now, in the future we can offer you exactly what you want.' This pits your wishful thinking against your better judgement. Either tie the future deal to the present agreement as one of its terms, or ignore it.

This chapter has looked at approaches to negotiating and some techniques that are useful in the negotiating process. Developing negotiating skills takes practice. Training, especially role play, is the best way to get practice. These important communication skills cannot easily be learnt out of a book. Talk to your line manager if you feel that you need more training in this area. You may find it useful to make notes on specific aspects of negotiating that you would like to develop in the action plan section of Chapter 10.

RECOMMENDED READING

- Communication and Negotiation (1992) Linda Puttnam and Michael Roloff, Sage, Newbury Park, California. For an overview of negotiating processes which includes discussion of more 'social' approaches, such as joint problem-solving.

- *It's a Deal: A practical negotiation handbook* (1989) Paul Steele, John Murphy and Richard Russill. One of several quick guides to business negotiating techniques which you will probably find on the business management shelves of most bookshops.

- *Negotiation in Social Conflict* (1993) Dean Pruitt and Peter Carnevale, Open University Press. Another overview of negotiating processes that includes more 'social' approaches.

9 Involving users

The aim of this chapter is to focus on the person needing care. In many ways, this chapter should be the first, not the last, in a book on business skills for care management. Business skills are not an end in themselves; unless care management activities produce concrete benefits in terms of the user's well-being and quality of life, there is no point to them.

There is, however, a value in using this chapter to draw together the topics discussed earlier, and to look back at them from the point of view of the person needing care. The chapter reviews major tensions between the social and economic objectives of care management, and provides a checklist to help you consider the ways in which users are involved in your day-to-day practice. The final section returns to the values which lie at the heart of community care services, whatever system is used to organise and pay for them.

QUESTIONS THIS CHAPTER WILL TRY TO ANSWER

- Why is it important to involve users in the business aspects of care management?
- In what ways could or should users become more involved?
- How does the development of business skills benefit people who need care?

INVOLVING THE PERSON
WHO NEEDS CARE

At the centre of the community care reforms is the person who needs care. The Government's stated objectives are to increase choice and self-determination, maintain independence, promote partnership between users and providers, and provide equal opportunities for all (*Policy Guidance*, para 3.3; see also pp 50–51, where these objectives are set out in full).

Throughout the previous chapters, it has been emphasised that there are tensions between these social objectives and the economic objectives of controlling costs and targeting services. Care management is an uncomfortable job at times, because front-line workers have to work with a number of paradoxes in the reformed system.

- Competition can be one way of increasing choice for users, but it can also lead to duplication, fragmentation or absence of services.

- In a 'free' market, there are many suppliers and many customers, so the balance of power between the parties is, in principle, equal. The social care market is a 'managed' market in which the local authority, not the user, is the customer. Without effective care management, the user has no power to influence purchasing decisions.

- Needs-led assessment takes place within cash limits, and it may be these limits, rather than users' perception of their needs, which decide what services care management staff can or cannot buy.

The purpose of developing business skills is not to turn care management into a business. It is to help you develop your ability to operate within the reformed market system, so that you are better equipped to help users get the best out of it, to recognise the opportunities that exist for doing this, and to work with and around the shortcomings that you come up against in practice. Your knowledge and skills – in understanding contracts, tailoring them to individual needs, working with budgets, ensuring quality and negotiating – help to give users protection against the weaknesses of the market system (for example unscrupulous providers, cut-price purchasing, competition pushing down quality as well as price).

At the same time, none of the social objectives listed on pages 50–51 can be achieved unless care management sets out to involve users. The checklist that follows aims to help you look at how users are involved in care management in your own authority. The questions concentrate on the business aspects that we have covered in earlier chapters.

Involving users at this level is, of course, only part of the picture. Care management objectives cannot be achieved without management support, adequate training for front-line workers and, most important of all, the involvement of users at a strategic level – through representative bodies such as users' groups – in the development of service specifications, contracts, quality assurance systems and the monitoring of providers' services.

To save space, the questions below refer only to users, but it is assumed that carers will be involved too where this is appropriate. In some cases, the carer may have to help or speak for a person who has difficulty in communicating.

INVOLVING USERS IN CARE MANAGEMENT: A GOOD PRACTICE AUDIT

Most questions require you to tick one of the boxes in the right-hand column, but for some, you may find it more helpful to make notes.

	OK/ Already do this	No/ Could do more
Eligibility for services		
■ Do you understand the range of services set out in the community care plan?	☐	☐
■ How do you make information about the community care plan available to users?		

Assessment

■ How are users given information about the assessment process?

■ What information is made available?

■ Have users been asked whether it is adequate?	☐	☐
■ Is the assessment process accessible to all users?	☐	☐

	OK/ Already do this	No/ Could do more

■ What do you do to make sure that users who cannot communicate easily have their say?

■ Do assessment procedures enable you to carry out an assessment **with** rather than **of** the user? ☐ ☐

■ Do you always get permission from users if you need to involve other professionals in the assessment? ☐ ☐

Care planning

■ Do you use a joint problem-solving approach to care planning whenever possible? ☐ ☐

■ Do you encourage users to specify their own outcomes wherever feasible? ☐ ☐

■ Do you always give users a copy of the care plan? ☐ ☐

Tailoring the contract to individual needs

■ Do you explain the contract to users? ☐ ☐

■ Is the user given clear information about the service specification? ☐ ☐

■ Is the user a party to the individual service contract? ☐ ☐

■ Do you explain what signing it means? ☐ ☐

■ Do you discuss with the user how you will specify individual care needs in the contract? ☐ ☐

■ How do you make sure that the care plan and individual service contract meet the cultural and/or religious needs of users from minority communities?

■ Are users always given the name of a key person to contact if they have any queries or difficulties with the service? ☐ ☐

Ensuring quality

■ What methods are used to gather users' and carers' views/experiences of care management?

	OK/ Already do this	No/ Could do more

■ What methods, formal and informal, are used to gather users' and carers' views/experiences of the services they receive?

■ Do these methods ensure that the views of all users, including people from black and ethnic minorities and those who cannot easily communicate, are included? ☐ ☐

■ Do you give users information about the quality standards or codes of practice of the services they receive? ☐ ☐

■ Do you make sure that they understand and can use the provider's complaints system? ☐ ☐

■ Do you ensure that users understand the social services complaints procedure? ☐ ☐

■ Do you support users wanting to make an appeal or complaint, or ask for a review, and try to allay any fears about being seen as a 'troublemaker'? ☐ ☐

■ Do you keep in touch with users' groups to get feedback about quality? ☐ ☐

■ Do procedures for reviewing the care plan fully involve users? ☐ ☐

Financial matters

■ Do you explain the purpose of the financial assessment to users and obtain their permission to ask questions about their finances? ☐ ☐

■ Do you carry out a financial assessment **with, for** or **of** the user?

■ Do you make sure that users have enough information about financial assessment, charging policies, eligibility criteria and welfare rights to make informed decisions about the care package? ☐ ☐

■ Do you fully discuss costs with the users, and creative ways of achieving their priorities within the resources available? ☐ ☐

Negotiating

- Do you always discuss with users what they hope
  to achieve before negotiating with others on their behalf? □ □
- Do you continually look for opportunities to involve users
  in negotiating where this is appropriate? □ □
- Do you make sure service users are fully aware that
  they can seek independent advice or the support of an
  advocate? □ □

Some of the issues raised in this checklist may be decided by management policies or procedures which are outside the control of care management staff. But there are bound to be small things that you can do as a front-line worker to find ways of increasing users' involvement in your own activities. Involving users doesn't have to take a lot of time or money; in the long term, it will cut down time and money wasted on inappropriate and inefficient services.

You may find it useful to make notes on ideas for involving users in the action plan section of the next chapter.

This chapter covers only one dimension of a much wider debate about how far the reformed community care system empowers users or disempowers them. There is no doubt that the reforms create opportunities for empowering some, although it may marginalise others. At the same time, giving front-line workers responsibility for buying care necessarily limits their role in helping and empowering clients and in acting as advocates for them. There is not the space here to go fully into the issues surrounding empowerment and advocacy, but the debate is an important one, for it is central to future decisions about how community care should develop. (See the suggestions in 'Recommended reading' if you would like to read more on these issues.)

Where do the business skills that we have discussed fit in with the rest of day-to-day practice? It is perhaps most helpful to think about business skills in care management as struts in the structure of the reformed community care system. They are not the only struts holding it up, but the system works much better if they are there. At the end of the day, as Malcolm Payne emphasises in *Social Work and Community Care*, what is most important is the 'glue' which keeps the whole structure together. That glue is the personal relationships, human qualities, caring skills and shared commitment of front-line workers to their clients, clients' families and carers, and to the values which underpin community care.

■ A commitment to ensure that all users and carers enjoy the same rights of citizenship as everyone else in the community, offering an equal access to service provision, irrespective of gender, race, or disability.

■ A respect for the independence of individuals and their right to self-determination and to take risks, minimising any restraint on that freedom of action.

■ A regard for the privacy of the individual, intruding no more than necessary to achieve the agreed purpose and guaranteeing confidentiality.

■ An understanding of the dignity and individuality of every user and carer.

■ A quest, within available resources, to maximise individual choice in the type of services on offer and the way in which those services are delivered.

■ A responsibility to provide services in a way that promotes the realisation of an individual's aspirations and abilities in all aspects of daily life.

Summary of Practice Guidance, para 81

RECOMMENDED READING

■ *The Community Care Handbook* (1995) Barbara Meredith, ACE Books.

■ *Community Care and Empowerment* (1993) Phyllida Parsloe and Olive Stevenson, Joseph Rowntree Foundation/Community Care.

■ *Social Work and Community Care* (1995) Malcolm Payne, Macmillan. Chapter 7 'Empowerment and advocacy for users' interests' provides an excellent review of current issues and recent research.

Official guidance referred to in this chapter

■ *Care Management and Assessment: Summary of Practice Guidance* (1991) HMSO.

■ *Community Care in the Next Decade and Beyond. Policy Guidance* (1990) HMSO.

■ *Purchase of Service: Practice Guidance and practice material for social services departments and other agencies* (1991) Department of Health Social Services Inspectorate, HMSO.

10 Where next?

Developing business skills in order to get the best out of the present system for service users is an ongoing process. In many ways this introductory guide has only scratched the surface: it isn't possible in a general guide to tackle the details of day-to-day procedures and practice in social services departments. To become more effective in the business aspects of care management, you will need to follow up and continue developing the knowledge and skills introduced here. The following action plan gives you a framework for further development.

ACTION PLAN

You may want to make notes on the action plan on pages 158–159 as you work through the chapters you have chosen to read. Or you may prefer to look back through the chapters that were most useful as you start to develop your action plan.

1 Read through the topics below, and tick the ones which you feel you need to find out more about or develop further. (You may find it helpful to look back to the Contents page for a fuller list of the topics covered in this book.)

2 For the topics that you have ticked, number your top six priorities.

3 When you have decided on your priorities, look at the suggestions at the end of the action plan and decide what action you will take for each one.

If possible, discuss your list of priorities with your line manager and find out what you can do to go further with these topics. Before you do this, look at each priority and decide what kind of action *you* think might help. For example, do you need:

■ more information?

■ more training?

■ guidance or action from management?

■ an opportunity to review, discuss or develop current practice?

■ something else?

WHO CAN HELP?

Your line manager is probably the best person to talk to first. If you want information or training on specific aspects of policy or practice in your own authority, consider the other people who may be able to provide it:

The contracts manager – any aspect of contracting arrangements; may also deal with accreditation system for approved providers.

Service planning/service development officers – community care plans, service specifications for contracts.

Quality assurance officer – any aspect of the social services department's quality assurance system, or systems for monitoring the quality of providers.

Social services registration and inspection unit – queries about the standards of service in residential homes.

Health authority – queries about the standards of service in nursing homes.

Consumer affairs/complaints officer – the social services department's complaints system, both informal queries or concerns and formal complaints from service users.

Finance officers – the financial assessment process, the social services department's charging arrangements, etc.

Training officer – advice or guidance on training needs and how they might be met.

Professional association or trade union representative – concerns about safe practice or professional standards in care management, if you feel these have not been addressed by management.

ACTION PLAN

Chapter topic	Need to know more/ do further training Please tick	Own queries, notes, comments
1 Care management – the background	☐	
2 How local authorities purchase care	☐	
3 Buying care to meet users' needs	☐	
4 Understanding contracts	☐	
5 Tailoring the contract to individual needs	☐	
6 Ensuring quality	☐	
7 Financial skills	☐	
8 Negotiating	☐	
9 Involving users	☐	

**Priorities
1–6**

☐

☐

☐

☐

☐

☐

☐

☐

Finally, don't overlook **providers**. Opportunities to talk to different types of independent provider can help you understand their view of the social care market, the difficulties they face, and ways in which you can work with them for the benefit of service users.

Use the plan below to list the priorities that you know it is feasible for you to tackle, and the action you will take. Set yourself a date to do it by.

ACTION TIMETABLE

Priority	Who can help	Action I will take	When I will do it by

Appendix 1

Checklist of resources for community care

The diagram on page 162 shows the range of care providers that might have an input into the care package for an older person, and other resources. You may find it useful to compare this with the resources available for your own area, or client group, or a particular client.

The list on pages 163–164 sets out the services for older people that may be available from different providers. Services are described in terms of what users and carers say they need, rather than using organisational definitions. You may find it useful to circle or highlight the resources that you might want to develop in your own area.

The pattern of providers varies widely from area to area, so you will need to investigate and develop your own checklist. You could consider doing this on a team or area basis if you do not already keep a directory of local provision.

If your authority has an accreditation system for independent providers, you will need to select providers from the approved list. You should be well informed about the range of services available from approved providers.

CARE PROVIDERS THAT MIGHT HAVE AN INPUT INTO THE CARE PACKAGE

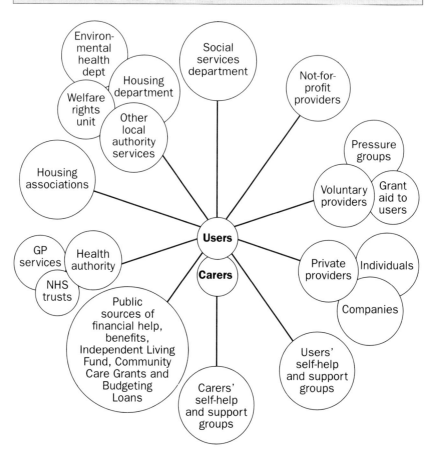

Source Adapted from *Care in the Community: Five years on* (1994)
Paul Cambridge et al, Arena.

CHECKLIST: SERVICES FOR OLDER PEOPLE AND POSSIBLE PROVIDERS

Services	Possible providers
Help in the home – domiciliary or home care services – help with nursing tasks, lifting, bathing, etc	*Social services, not-for-profit, voluntary or private agency* *Community nurse, private nursing agency*
Day centres	*Social services, voluntary organisation (eg Age Concern), community centre*
Residential homes	*Social services, private individual or company, not-for-profit or voluntary organisation*
Nursing homes	*Private individual or company, voluntary organisation*
Equipment and adaptations to improve the home environment	*Occupational therapist, voluntary organisation (eg Care and Repair)*
Laundry service	*Social services, health authority, private laundry*
Respite care in the home	*Social services, private agency, voluntary organisation (eg Crossroads)*
Help with transport, information about transport schemes	*Social services, Motability, Dial-a-Ride, other voluntary organisation*
Information and advice about welfare rights, availability of advocacy, etc	*Local authority welfare rights unit, voluntary organisation (eg Citizens Advice Bureau, Age Concern)*
Advocacy	*Advocacy schemes, voluntary organisations (eg Age Concern)*
Users' and carers' self-help or support groups	*Run by social services, health service or voluntary organisation (eg Stroke Club, Alzheimer's Disease Society, Carers National Association)*
Interpreting and advocacy services for black and ethnic minority users	*Social services, health authority, voluntary organisation*
Specialised services for black and ethnic minority users (day care, lunch clubs, etc)	*Social services, voluntary organisation*

Information about sheltered housing, specially adapted housing schemes, etc	*Housing department, housing association*
Advice or help with housing needs, repairs, maintenance, home improvement grants, etc	*Housing or environmental health department, voluntary organisation, eg Care and Repair*
Health advice and medical or nursing care in the home	*GP, community nurse, health visitor – some health visitors specialise in working with older people*
Advice and counselling from specialist nurses (eg for stoma care, diabetes, cancer)	*Hospital, community nursing service, Macmillan or Marie Curie nurses*
Advice, support, help for a specific disability or illness (eg Alzheimer's disease, HIV/AIDS, sensory impairment)	*Specialist local and national organisations (eg Alzheimer's Disease Society, Terrence Higgins Trust, Royal National Institute for the Blind/Deaf, etc)*
Physiotherapy, speech therapy, help with rehabilitation (eg after a stroke)	*Via GP, hospital, or rehabilitation unit*
Foot care, help with nail-cutting	*Chiropodist via GP or community nurse, or private*
Dietary advice	*Hospital or community dietician service*
Respite care away from home	*Social services, hospital, private or voluntary residential or nursing home*
Community dental services	*Via GP or health authority*
Training for users and/or family carers on a range of tasks such as safe lifting, giving injections and other medication, promoting continence, etc. Loan of short-term nursing equipment, etc	*Community nursing services, community occupational therapist*
Assessment of incontinence problems, practical help and advice	*Incontinence adviser, community nurse, health visitor*
Care at home for someone who is terminally ill	*Community nurse, Macmillan nurse, hospice day care*

Source Adapted from *Caring in a Crisis: What to do and who to turn to* (1995) Marina Lewycka, ACE Books.

Appendix 2

Sample service specification
for domiciliary care services

Source *Guidance on Contracting for Domiciliary and Day Care Services* (1995) Association of Metropolitan Authorities, Association of County Councils, Association of Directors of Social Services, published by Local Government Management Board.

1 Care principles

General: The approach to all people who need domiciliary care services will incorporate the general principles that those involved in the assessment and provision of services in service users' homes will in all cases:

■ treat people as individuals and promote each person's dignity, privacy and independence;

■ acknowledge that all care workers are visitors in the service user's home, and should act accordingly;

■ acknowledge and respect people's gender, sexual orientation, age, ability, race, religion, culture and lifestyle;

■ give service users and their carers the maximum possible choice of services within available resources to meet their needs;

■ recognise the right of service users to exercise the maximum possible control over the services they receive;

■ involve service users, carers and their representatives in the planning of services individually and collectively;

■ provide support for carers, whether relatives or friends, and recognise the rights of other family members;

- recognise that people's needs and their support networks may change over time, and ensure that services are able to respond sensitively and flexibly;

- plan and provide services in partnership with users, carers and other independent and statutory agencies, to ensure good working relationships and a co-ordinated approach to meeting needs.

2 Service sought

Authorities will wish to consider for themselves what other elements to include in this section to reflect more closely local policies and priorities. They will be mindful of negotiations with Health Authorities on their respective responsibilities.

2.1 Personal care

Personal care may include skills development (see below). The tasks undertaken will include those which could be given by family carers. It excludes nursing care which is the responsibility of the Health Service.

The services to be provided will include, but are not confined to:

- Assisting the service user to get up or go to bed. This service is time sensitive and should be undertaken within half an hour of a time specified by the user.

- Washing, bathing, hair care, denture and mouth care, hand and fingernail care, foot care (but nothing which requires a state registered chiropodist).*

- Assisting the user with:
  - dressing and undressing;
  - toileting, including necessary cleaning and safe disposal of waste;
  - eating and drinking, including associated kitchen cleaning and hygiene;
  - attending day care, hospital appointments, etc;
  - shopping and handling their own money, including accompanying the service user to the shops;
  - dealing with correspondence;

---

* Editor's note: Local authorities normally have detailed protocols on foot care which will be referred to in an actual contract specification.

– taking medication which has been prescribed to them [the local authority and health authority will have specific locally acceptable policy and procedures in this area].

2.2 Cleaning and housecare

Cleaning the home, which may include vacuuming, sweeping, washing up, housecare polishing, cleaning floors and windows, bathrooms, kitchens, toilets etc, using appropriate domestic equipment and appliances as available:

- tidying the home;

- making beds and changing bed linen;

- lighting fires, boilers etc;

- disposing of household and personal rubbish;

- cleaning areas used or fouled by pets; arranging their feeding, exercising and grooming;

- assisting with the consequences of household emergencies including liaison with local contractors;

- assisting the service user with food or drink preparation;

- shopping, collecting pensions, benefits or prescriptions, paying bills for service users or other simple errands.

2.3 Laundry services

These may comprise one or more of the following components:

- As part of a personal or domestic care package to include: laundering clothes and household linen (including fouled linen) using either the service user's own equipment or a launderette according to the service user's choice; hand washing; airing, drying, ironing, storage and mending.

- As part of a 'Community Laundry' service, provided for a number of users. The service shall include collection, sorting, sluicing, laundering, drying, folding, ironing and return of laundry in clean bags to the user's home or other specified point (within agreed timescales). The service shall include the provision of all laundry bags, equipment and labour.

2.4 Shopping services

Community shopping services available to a number of service users must ensure:

- service users are assisted to make informed choices;

- systems for ordering goods that are easy to use;

- the service promotes choice of branded and fresh goods, and can provide for people with special dietary needs or cultural requirements;

- the total cost of orders is advised to service users before the order is confirmed;

- delivery is within (a specified period/half an hour) of the time agreed with the service user;

- goods delivered are fresh and in good condition; frozen goods are frozen, and chilled goods cold, throughout the purchase and delivery period;

- frozen and chilled goods are unpacked and stored to the service user's satisfaction if required;

- itemised receipts are supplied, and methods of payment for the goods are agreed with each service user;

- the service will establish and maintain a system for the supply of substitutes agreeable to the service user when ordered items cannot be supplied.

2.5 Skills development

Providers may seek to assist the service user to develop or maintain their own skills in any of the areas covered in personal or domestic specifications or this may be specified as part of an individual's package of care, eg for service users with learning disabilities.

2.6 Focused visiting services

These services:

- concentrate on the social need of the service user rather than tasks to be performed;

- are preventative rather than reactive and contribute to an 'early warning' system for care managers;

- may be 'pop in', checking on someone's continuing wellbeing, or 'befriending' in nature, to alleviate isolation.

2.7 Other

Authorities may wish to purchase or encourage, through core funding or grant aid, other services such as garden maintenance, home decoration, or simple household odd jobs. Specifications should be designed locally to ensure accessibility, affordability and reliability.

3 Priority for service

Local authorities should set out here or refer to their eligibility criteria for receipt of service. This will serve a number of purposes:

■ service specifications should give service providers some indication of the potential marker;

■ they should give service users clear messages as to whether they qualify or not;

■ if the service provider is to take direct referrals and assess for service, for example for non-complex care, then they need a clear steer as to who will qualify.

4 Recruitment and training

Vetting and selection of staff or volunteers: The service provider will be expected to have a recruitment or selection policy and process which takes account of all current legislation, including equal opportunities legislation. The policy will cover recruitment, advertising and interviewing. It will also establish the competencies and qualifications of new workers and ensure that written references are routinely obtained before new staff begin work on the contract.

The service provider will have a suitable induction and training programme in place to ensure that all staff have a good understanding of the needs of service users, recognise their rights of choice and control, and have an aptitude and capacity for the work. The service provider will have suitable arrangements to identify and provide for ongoing training needs. The cost of training including coverage for absence needs to be recognised as an essential overhead to quality services.

Written arrangements must exist and records be kept relating to management and support for all staff involved in the provision of the service, to ensure that work is carried out correctly and good practice maintained.

Service purchasers should recognise the need for effective management in domiciliary care provision, as the role requires a wide range of skills, abilities and dedication.

The service provider should provide all staff with written information on their employment status, legal and insurance situation, job description, standards to be attained, agency policies and practices, and complaints, grievance and disciplinary procedures. The service provider must ensure that care staff are adequately insured. Arrangements will vary depending on whether the service provider is an agent (using self employed or volunteer staff) or principal (employing care workers direct).

5 General conduct

The service provider will ensure that service users and carers are treated with courtesy and respect at all times and in a manner which enhances their dignity and self-respect. Domiciliary care staff are guests in the service user's home and should act as such, for example, respecting the service user's views in respect of smoking.

Misconduct: Any allegation of misconduct which is detrimental to the well-being of the service user will be investigated under the agreed complaints procedure and may result in the termination of the whole contract or the ISC. Misconduct includes the following:

- fraud or theft;
- physical or mental abuse, including threatening behaviour, physical restraint, deprivation of care or harassment;
- any type of sexual exploitation;
- neglect of service user requirements.

Gifts and inducements: The service provider will have a written policy on the receipt of gifts. Service providers or their staff must not accept financial inducements, seek to be made the beneficiary of a will or obtain any other financial benefits from the user.

Service users' moneys: Service providers must not become involved with the financial affairs of the service user without the explicit agreement of the purchaser. This would exclude assistance with simple monetary transactions. The service provider shall have a written policy on handling service users' money which makes clear the acceptable limits of their involvement.

6 Confidentiality

Service providers must have a written policy on confidentiality. This should ensure that personal information disclosed to the service provider in the course of their work must be treated as confidential and should only be disclosed with the consent of the person concerned, unless that person is at risk. The need to disclose information to other providers for the benefit of the user should be considered and should follow locally agreed protocols.

7 Service users at risk

The service provider must immediately inform the purchaser if they have any reason to believe that a service user or carer is at risk through self neglect, or as a result of their behaviour or lifestyle, or because of the actions or behaviour of others. Where the service user is a family with young children existing policies or notification of suspected abuse must be followed. Police checks are also required where young children are on the premises.

The service provider will have clear arrangements covering what to do in an emergency, including arrangements for informing social services. The provider will instruct all staff on emergency procedures, including what to do in a domestic emergency, if the service user fails to answer or is suspected of being missing, injured, ill or dead.

8 Quality

8.1 Outcomes sought

Both purchasers and providers must be clear what outcomes are being sought for each individual service user. Normally these outcomes will be specified in the service user's individual care plan. Where widely accessed services are purchased the aims of the service should make clear the general outcomes sought.

8.2 Service aims

The service should:

- provide reliable practical support which helps people increase control over their daily lives;

- prevent admission to residential or nursing home care when the person wishes to stay in their own home;

- assist carers to continue to provide care;

- provide short-term help to assist rehabilitation;

- enable discharge from hospital to take place without delay;

- ensure that no one referred to the service is left at risk without the offer of services;

- offer planned transfer to other services when needed.

8.3 User centred services

The services to be provided to service users and carers will be those specified by the care manager (or other purchaser representative) in accordance with the individual's care plan, and these may change over time; requests from users or carers for tasks additional to those agreed should be responded to with sensitivity and flexibility within the terms of the contract and the agency's sphere of competence.

The service provider will consult with the service user or carer on the detail of how the work is to be carried out within the individual service contract, and every effort will be made to meet their preferences. Any difficulties or conflicts which cannot be resolved will be referred to the care manager for resolution.

Service providers will carry out their work in a manner which recognises their role as part of a network maintaining the service user's well-being and independence. The service provider will:

- maintain liaison with the service purchaser and initiate contact when significant changes in circumstances occur or appear likely, or where there appears to be a danger that agreed objectives will not be met;

- contribute to reviews;

- maintain appropriate contact with the user's family and other supporters;

- give active consideration to the user's or carer's information needs relating to, for example, benefits, services or other aspects of daily living, and facilitate access to such information wherever possible;
- maintain individual care programmes and suitable records where appropriate.

8.4 Quality assurance

Service providers will need to demonstrate that the standards of service required are being delivered and the care needs of service users met. They should have quality assurance systems in place which are user-centred, approved by the service purchaser and which ensure effective working practices appropriate to the needs and wishes of users.

Compliance with quality assurance standards will be ensured through local accreditation arrangements where evidence of systems will be required.

8.5 Monitoring requirements (eg returns and frequency)

Service purchasers should concentrate on what is required to ensure contract compliance. Information which is not in or related to the contract should not, as a rule, be sought. Purchasers must be clear about the kinds of information they require, its frequency and use.

8.6 User feedback

- There should be a system for monitoring service user satisfaction.
- The service provider will also have a system for recording and dealing with complaints which is acceptable to the purchaser.
- The service provider should indicate what arrangements they have for involving service users and carers in planning their service.
- The service user will have access to the purchaser's own complaints procedure.

9 Legislative

Although the restrictions governing compulsory competitive tendering do not apply to the writing of the specification, two areas of legislation are important:

i) Health and safety

Provider responsibilities

The service provider will have a written health and safety policy. The provider will maintain good practice in the areas of health and safety at work, including manual handling, food handling, personal hygiene and the control of infection for all staff providing services under a contract with the purchaser.

Provision/use of equipment

All equipment belonging to the user and used by the service provider must be maintained in a safe condition at the service user's expense. Equipment that appears in any way to be faulty must not be used until it has been checked, and if necessary repaired, by a qualified person.

Transport

Where service users are to be transported as part of the service, eg taken shopping, particular care should be taken to ensure that adequate insurance arrangements are in place.

ii) Equal opportunities in service delivery

The alternative to including reference to equal opportunities and service delivery throughout the specification is to make specific reference to an equal opportunities standard, which may also be used as part of the accreditation criteria. An example of such a standard may read:

> 'Services should be delivered in a non discriminatory and non patronising and professional manner, by well trained and courteous staff. Service users should be treated with dignity and respect, and staff delivering the service should be acquainted with any special requirements associated with the EC guide in food preparation, toilet and washing, hair care, dress and religious needs and customs. Wherever possible the provider should endeavour to ensure, whilst keeping within the law, that where the user has preference to be cared for by staff of certain gender, ethnic or religious cultural group, where this arises from recognised religious or cultural needs, then those

needs should be respected, and appropriate staff with the necessary skills allocated to provide the service.'

It is important to note that any statement on equal opportunities and service delivery should not contravene the law.

EC legislation that purchasers need to consider

The directive which became binding on member states in July 1993 was translated into UK law on 13 January 1994 through statutory instrument no 233a the Public Services Contract Regulations 1993. The law has a two tier application with some services being classed as priority services (Annexe A services) and therefore subject to the full procurement regime and some services being classed as residual (Annexe B) services and therefore only subject in part to the law at present. Health and social services are currently classed as Annexe B services which means that in addition to complying with the treaty of Rome they need only comply with the regulations relating to contract specification and publish contract award notices in the official journal of the European Community (OJEC). However, it should be noted that the treaty of Rome requires all specifications to be non discriminatory in terms of their application across member states, thus eg: it would be discriminatory to state that a service provider is required to have a British standard kite mark without specifying its European equivalent.

The financial thresholds for application of the law are that the estimated value of the contract is 2,000 ECU or more, £149,728.00. It is the aggregate value of all individual contracts that determines the financial threshold not the individual contracts per se. Thus, all local authorities will be subject to the regulations in terms of social care purchasing.

Whilst health and social services currently fall into Annexe B it is possible that these services will become subject to full regime following a review to be completed by June 1996 and move into Annexe A.

10 Information for service users

Providers must ensure that service users receive clear information about their service. This should include:

- when the service will start;
- how long it will last, or is likely to last;

- how much it will cost and what the arrangements are for collecting charges;
- an individual agreement about the tasks to be done for each person;
- wherever possible, who their helpers will be (names of carers);
- a telephone number for help in an emergency;
- how to make a complaint, to whom, and how it will be handled;
- how to initiate a review of their care arrangements.

Appendix 3

Sample individual service contract (ISC) for the purchase of domiciliary care services

Source *Guidance on Contracting for Domiciliary and Day Care Services* (1995) Association of Metropolitan Authorities, Association of County Councils, Association of Directors of Social Services, published by Local Government Management Board.

Contract Number .... / .... (Team)

This ISC is for the purchase of Domiciliary Care Services in accordance with the conditions of the Pre Placement Agreement with Service Provider. The terms of the Service Agreement, to the extent that they are not inconsistent within this ISC, are deemed to be incorporated in this ISC

Service Provider Details

Contact Reference ....

Address ....

Telephone No ....

Service Purchaser Details

District ....

Address ....

Responsible worker ....

Telephone No ....

Case Number ....

Service User Details (Please use block capitals)

Surname .... Forenames ....

Address ....

Title ....
(Mr, Mrs, Miss or Other)

The ISC shall commence on .... day .... month, 199

OR in week commencing ...., and shall continue until .... day

.... month 199 , or until further notice

* Summary of Services to be Provided

Service (List services with different unit costs on separate lines)	Per Week		
	Total Units	Unit Cost	Total Cost

Total Cost

* These Services may be amended by verbal agreement in accordance with the conditions
of the Pre Placement Agreement and recorded on the Amendment to ISC as attached.

Income Collection Details (if any)

Delete if not applicable

This ISC, dated .... is signed and agreed by the following:

Name .... Designation .... on behalf of Council

Name .... by/or on behalf of Service User

Name .... Designation .... by the Service Provider

Please see further conditions over

Amendments to ISC

Local Authority Name ....

Service User Name .... Contract Number ....

Provider Name .... Case Number ....

PART A PERMANENT CHANGE OF SERVICE

The following services have increased/decreased*

Enter service details that have changed, eg hours/days. (If service is to be provided on different day(s) please show decrease then increase.)

COST DETAILS

Budget Code

Change of Service User Contribution

PART B SUSPENSION OF SERVICE

Please complete this section if service is to be temporarily suspended.

Start date of suspension (after normal notice) ....

End date of suspension (if known) ....

	COST DETAILS

PART C TEMPORARY CHANGE TO SERVICE

State whether increase or decrease.

Start date ....

End date ....

	COST DETAILS

PART D TERMINATION OF ISC

Termination date ....

Reason for termination ....

	COST DETAILS

This contract amendment to the ISC No .... date .... is made on behalf of all interested parties.

Signed on behalf of the Service Purchaser ....

Service Provider ....

Service User ....

About Age Concern

Business Skills for Care Management: A guide to costing, contracting and negotiating is one of a wide range of publications produced by Age Concern England, the National Council on Ageing. Age Concern England is actively engaged in training, information provision, fundraising and campaigning for retired people and those who work with them, and also in the provision of products and services such as insurance for older people.

A network of over 1,400 local Age Concern groups, with the support of around 250,000 volunteers, aims to improve the quality of life of older people and develop services appropriate to local needs and resources. These include advice and information, day care, visiting services, transport schemes, clubs, and specialist facilities for older people who are physically and mentally frail.

Age Concern England is a registered charity dependent on public support for the continuation and development of its work.

Age Concern England
1268 London Road
London SW16 4ER
Tel: 0181-679 8000

Age Concern Scotland
113 Rose Street
Edinburgh EH2 3DT
Tel: 0131-220 3345

Age Concern Cymru
4th Floor
1 Cathedral Road
Cardiff CF1 9SD
Tel: 01222 371566

Age Concern Northern Ireland
3 Lower Crescent
Belfast BT7 1NR
Tel: 01232 245729

Publications from
AGE CONCERN BOOKS

Professional handbooks

The Community Care Handbook: The reformed system explained
Barbara Meredith
Written by one of the country's leading experts, the new edition of this hugely successful handbook provides a comprehensive overview of the first two years of implementation of the community care reforms and examines how the system has evolved. This second edition is essential reading for all those keen to keep up to date and fully informed on the ever-changing community care picture.

£13.99   0–86242–171–3

Residents' Money: A guide to good practice in care homes
People who live in a residential or nursing home have the same right as everyone else to spend their own money as they wish. This book sets out the basic principles involved in enabling older people to manage their own money and make their own choices. Essential reading for care home managers, care workers and relatives.

£6.95   0–86242–205–1

Health Care in Residential Homes
Dr Anne Roberts
Written in response to widespread demand for a book on this subject, *Health Care in Residential Homes* provides clear and straightforward information for managers and other care staff on maintaining residents' health and dealing with their health problems. Topics covered include the common illnesses of later life, the medicines prescribed, health promo-

tion, what to do in an emergency and coping with terminal illness and bereavement.

£14.95   0–86242–156–X

Health and Safety in Care Homes: A practical guide

Sarah Tullett

This book is a complete reference manual to health and safety in care homes. It contains full coverage of issues such as UK and European Union legislation, risk assessment, equipment and hazardous substances – all the while encouraging managers and proprietors to assess their own health and safety provision and adapt the information provided to their own situations.

£11.99   0–86242–186–1

CareFully: A handbook for home care assistants

Lesley Bell

This highly acclaimed and accessible guide provides practical advice on the day-to-day tasks home care assistants encounter and addresses issues such as legal responsibilities and emotional involvement.

£10.99   0–86242–129–2

Managing CareFully: A guide for managers of home care services

Lesley Bell

A follow-up to the immensely successful *CareFully*, this book provides all the advice and guidance that those responsible for managing home care services need. As well as providing detailed background information to the community care reforms, this book also explores practical issues such as assessing local needs, selecting staff, handling clients' money and responding to clients' changing needs.

£14.99   0–86242–185–3

If you would like to order any of these titles, please write to the address below, enclosing a cheque or money order for the appropriate amount made payable to Age Concern England. Credit card orders may be made on 0181-679 8000.

Mail Order Unit
Age Concern England
1268 London Road
London SW16 4ER

Information factsheets

Age Concern England produces over 30 factsheets on a variety of subjects. Among these the following titles may be of interest to readers of this book:

Factsheet 6 *Finding help at home*

Factsheet 10 *Local authority charging procedures for residential and nursing home care*

Factsheet 32 *Disability and ageing: Your rights to social services*

To order factsheets

Single copies are available free on receipt of a 9″ × 6″ sae. If you require a selection of factsheets or multiple copies totalling more than five, charges will be given on request.

A complete set of factsheets is available in a ring binder at a cost of £36, which includes the first year's subscription. The current cost for annual subscription for subsequent years is £17. There are different rates of subscription for people living outside the UK.

Briefing papers

The following Age Concern England briefing papers may also be of interest to readers:

Local authority assessment procedures for community care services (ref 2095).
Treatment of the former home as capital for people in residential and nursing homes (ref 1195).

Information about transfer of assets by older people with respect to local authority charging procedures for residential and nursing home care (ref 2495).
Local authority charging procedures for residential and nursing home care: liable relatives and occupational pensions (ref 1395)

For further information, or to order factsheets or briefing papers, write to:

Information and Policy Department
Age Concern England
1268 London Road
London SW16 4ER

Index